THE LAST
CHRISTIAN
GENERATION

THE LAST CHRISTIAN GENERATION

Josh McDowell
David H. Bellis

GREEN KEY BOOKS

Holiday, Florida

Published by Green Key Books
2514 Aloha Place
Holiday, Florida 34691

Cataloging-in-Publication Data available upon request.

Printed in the United States of America.

06 07 08 7 6 5 4 3 2 1

Table of Contents

Acknowledgements

I would like to thank the following people for their collaborative assistance on this book:

Dave Bellis, my friend and colleague for twenty-nine years, for being my co-author. While Dave wrote and authored the first draft and the many edited drafts after that in a collaborative effort with me to complete the entire project, he requested that his name not appear on the front cover. He says he doesn't need the recognition since he doesn't aspire to author any books on his own. But I certainly recognize both his passionate ownership of this message and his writing skills to deliver this work to you.

Bob Hostetler for editing the first draft. His incredible talent and passionate heart for process-driven ministry is unsurpassed.

Tom Williams for editing the manuscript in which he applied his intellect, writing skills, and heart to this work. Tom's collaboration with Dave throughout the process has brought clarity to this all-important message.

Eric Bolger, Mark Rapinchuk, Sean McDowell, Chris Sleath, David Hone, and Solomon Mekonnen for critiquing the manuscript and providing insight, correctives, and valuable input to make a clearer and more effective work.

Becky Bellis for her tireless effort when inputting the manuscript into the computer in its many drafts and revisions and keeping it all straight.

Krissi Castor of Green Key Books for her excellent copyediting of the manuscript. Her talents, efficiency and attention to detail made the manuscript a better work.

And finally, to Lynnda Speer and Pete Castor of Green Key who caught the vision for this message and championed it to bookstores, churches, and families throughout the country. You have become a valued partner in equipping and empowering this generation to become true followers of Christ.

Josh McDowell

ONE
The Reality

"I realize the title of this book may be shocking. But the decision to call this *The Last Christian Generation* was not made lightly nor was it done for sensationalism. I sincerely believe unless something is done now to change the spiritual state of our young people—*you* will become the last Christian generation!"

Josh McDowell

Marsha hugged her son as he prepared to leave. "It's been nice having you home again, honey," she said.

"Yeah, Greg," his father Mike echoed. "It really has been good." He stepped in for a hug. "I miss the weekends as a family, going to church and all. But I assume you've found a church home there in the college area by now, haven't you, son?"

Greg swung an arm through a loop of his backpack. "Well, Dad, not really," he said hesitantly. "Being a first-year college student is tough, so I've been really busy."

Sarah, Greg's sixteen-year-old sister, handed him his duffle bag. "Is college really that hard?"

"Well, I wouldn't say hard, really. You just keep busy, you know?"

Mike clamped a hand on Greg's shoulder. "If you're too busy to be in church, son, I think you might be too busy."

"Well," Greg responded, "your kind of church just isn't my thing anymore, Dad. I've got some friends and we do a group study once a week and that's enough for me."

"I'd rather do things with my friends, too," Sarah added. "Church is a bore."

"Sarah!" Marsha said. "That's a terrible thing to say!"

"Well, it's true!" Sarah said.

"She's right, Mom," Greg said. "Church just doesn't cut it for me anymore."

"Honey, don't say that." Marsha touched her son on the arm. "That college isn't turning you against God, is it?"

"No, Mom," Greg chuckled, "I'm just rethinking a lot of things. God is still important to me, I just believe some different things from you guys, that's all." He adjusted the weight of the backpack. "Hey, I've got to get going."

Greg moved on out the door as Sarah helped him with his things. Marsha and Mike stepped onto the porch and watched their son walk toward the car.

"We'll be praying for you, son," Mike called.

"Thanks, Dad," Greg responded with a chuckle.

Marsha and Mike watched in silence as he backed down the drive and waved to them as he drove away. "I hope we're not losing our son," Marsha said.

Mike nodded. "I hope we're not losing our son *and* our daughter."

Are Our Kids Embracing True Christianity?

If I hear one dominating and recurring theme among the many church leaders and families I come in contact with, it's fear. Some can express their fear. Others can't quite put it into words. But most admit to a fear, deep down, that their kids, having been raised in Christian families and having spent their childhood and teenage years in the church, will, nonetheless, walk away unchanged. They fear that they are the last Christian generation and that their children will depart from the true faith.

That fear has become a reality. In past years, between fifty-five percent (55%) and sixty-six percent (66%) of churched young people have said that the church will play a part in their lives when they leave home. Now only thirty-three percent (33%) of churched youth say that![1] This is consistent with what various denominational leaders have confessed to me. Many have estimated that between sixty-nine percent (69%) and ninety-four percent (94%) of their young people are leaving the traditional church after high school ... and very few are returning.

It's not that churches and Christian families haven't recognized that we're losing our young people and haven't tried to do something about it. During the 1970's and 1980's, significant numbers of Christian parents began removing their children from the public school system in an attempt to salvage their kids. The hope was that a Christian school education would somehow undergird their children with a biblical worldview. Today, there are over twelve thousand Christian schools in the United States. But what are the results?

For nineteen years, the Nehemiah Institute in Lexington, Kentucky, has been offering Christian schools what is called PEERS testing. This is to identify a young person's views in five areas: Politics, Economics, Education, Religion, and Social issues (PEERS). The test is framed to grade a student according to one of four worldviews— Biblical Theism, Moderate Christian, Secular Humanism, and Socialism.

The Nehemiah Institute has offered a valuable service in providing this type of testing to over 20,000 students from one thousand schools (see *www.NehemiahInstitute. com*). Christian parents have even tested their young people who attend public school. You would probably not be surprised to learn that eighty-five percent (85%) of youth from Christian homes that attend public schools do not embrace a biblical worldview. But what of students in Christian schools? While these students scored slightly higher than their counterparts attending public schools, only six percent (6%) of students embraced a Biblical Theism Worldview.[2] It is clear we have all but lost our young people to a godless culture.

That is not to say, however, that our young people are rebelling against God. In fact, in many ways, today's youth are just as promising and as spiritually inclined as any generation. Perhaps even more so. Studies show they possess an impressive set of priorities:

- 65% want a close relationship with God;[3]
- 49% want to make a difference in the world;[4]

- 79% consider having close personal friends as a high-priority goal for their future.[5]

Today's youth seem to be just as interested in God and just as passionate about spiritual things as any generation. For more than a decade, young people have been the most spiritually interested individuals in America. Their interest is not in question at all. But the fundamental question is: "How are they forming their view of God? And what brand of religion are they adopting?"

A large proportion of our young people would echo Greg's remark at the beginning of this chapter: "God is still important to me, I just believe some different things from you."

What are these differences? For starters:

- 63% don't believe Jesus is the Son of the one true God;
- 58% believe all faiths teach equally valid truths;
- 51% don't believe Jesus rose from the dead;
- 65% don't believe Satan is a real entity;
- 68% don't believe the Holy Spirit is a real entity.[6]

In other words, our kids are departing from the faith of their fathers...and mothers. They are believing "some different things from you and me." Much of what they believe about Christianity, truth, reality, and the church comes from a distorted view they have gleaned from the world around them. It's not that they haven't embraced a version of Christianity; it's simply that the version they believe in is not built on the true foundation of what biblical Christianity is all about.

But it's more than a matter of the things they believe. Those differences in belief make a world of difference in the kind of lives they lead. You see, when our view of the truth becomes distorted, then how we view God, ourselves, and others is profoundly affected, too. And, sooner or later, what we believe will govern how we think and act.

Research shows that when young people lack a basic biblical belief system, it negatively affects their attitudes. As a result they are:

- 225% more likely to be angry with life
- 216% more likely to be resentful
- 210% more likely to lack purpose in life
- 200% more likely to be disappointed in life.[7]

The research also shows that our young people's failure to adopt a foundational Christian belief system negatively impacts their behavior:

- 48% more likely to cheat on an exam
- 200% more likely to steal
- 200% more likely to physically hurt someone
- 300% more likely to use illegal drugs
- 600% more likely to attempt suicide.[8]

The above quoted research tells us that when our young people are not grounded upon the foundational truth of what Christianity really is, they are two times, three times, and *six* times more likely to engage in "un-Christlike" and destructive behavior. And studies show this to be precisely the situation we have today. The Josephson Institute on Ethics' report entitled, "The Ethics of American Youth," underscores this reality.

In the last 12 months who...

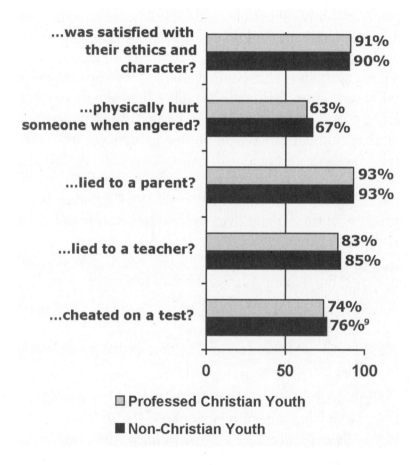

According to this study, there is no more than a four percent (4%) difference between the attitudes and actions of professing Christian youth and non-Christian young people.

Isn't something terribly wrong with this picture? Studies show that the majority of our young people want a close relationship with God and perhaps are more inclined toward spiritual things than the previous generation. And yet their beliefs and lifestyles are inconsistent with what you and I would consider to be true Christianity. Wouldn't true followers of Christ believe that Jesus is the Son of the one true God? Wouldn't they say that Jesus bodily rose from the dead? Wouldn't they accept that the Holy Spirit is a real person? And would they lie to their teachers and parents, cheat on tests, and steal from others? The cornerstones of the Christian faith is that the power of Christ so transforms a person that he or she begins acting Christlike. That is what a Christian is—a person who thinks and lives in the likeness of his or her Lord, Jesus Christ.

A ground-breaking study by George Barna divided professed born-again Christians into two categories:

1. Those who believe in Christ, but their lives don't reflect Christlikeness; and
2. Those who believe in Christ and live a Christlike life.

His research showed that ninety-eight percent (98%) of professed born-again young people do "believe in Christ," *but they do not reflect Christlike attitudes or actions!*[10]

What has happened? Why does the Christianity that so many of our young people, and even adults, are adopting make so little difference in their lives? Is it because they are not attending enough church services and Christian events or that there are not enough seminars and resources available in the form of books, training, or curriculum to teach them the truth about Christianity? Although it may sound harsh, I'm afraid George Barna is right when he says:

> Nothing is more numbing to the Church than the fact that it is mired in a rut of seemingly unfathomable depths. The various creative approaches attempted over the course of this decade have drawn much attention but produced little, if any, transformational impact…although many people attend a church, few Americans are committed to *being* the Church.[11]

We haven't lacked creative resources or high-impact Christian events over the last decade. We are inundated with books, courses, and events. And while these efforts have been worthwhile, because some people's lives have been transformed by the power of God, for some reason we're losing more ground with this new generation of young people than we are gaining.

What Do We Need?

Paul the Apostle said that when a person has a real encounter with the true God, that relationship will transform him or her into a new creation: "Whoever is a believer in Christ is a new creation. The old way of living has disappeared. A new way of living has come into existence" (2 Corinthians 5:17, GWT).

The obvious but, nonetheless, shocking truth is that we are not seeing the majority of our churched youth transformed by the power of God. There are exceptions, of course, but the majority of our young people appear neither to understand who the true God is nor the true meaning of Christianity. It is evident that the Church and Christian families are failing to lead them into a transforming experience with God!

"Wait a minute, McDowell," you might say. "We are still presenting the gospel message to our young people as we always have. Christ is as relevant as he has ever been. If they're not experiencing him, it's not our fault!"

This book isn't about casting blame or trying to determine who is at fault for the things that are happening—or not happening—among our young people. I am wholly uninterested in making anyone feel worse for the spiritual and moral state of our young people. It is abundantly clear that our own "Christian" young people are walking away from the church in alarming numbers. And I'm sure you'll agree that whatever or whoever is the cause, we all want to find a way to keep your generation from being the last Christian generation.

In this book, we want to come to grips with the impact of a cultural view of Christianity, truth, reality, and the church that has completely distorted how our kids understand God. Yes, churches and families may present the truth of Christ to our young people, but most kids will interpret such presentations through the distorted prisms they've adopted from the culture around them. And unless we recognize how our kids process the gospel through these distortions—and then re-think how we introduce them to Christ—they may never understand or experience the true God who transforms lives!

In the chapters that follow, we want to identify the distorted views of the faith that our young people are adopting, but we will go beyond that. We will also examine what it will take to correct their distorted views of God so that we can rebuild the true foundations of the faith within this generation, and by God's grace, a new generation of true Christians will emerge. We do not use the word "rebuild" lightly. It is true that the foundation of Christianity does not need to be rebuilt because "Christ Jesus himself is the cornerstone" (Ephesians 2:20, GWT). And Christ does not need to be modernized to make him relevant—he is as relevant as ever before. But the issue here is that the majority of our young people lack a relationship with spiritual mentors who are models of Christlikeness, and these youth are building their faith and lives on a false foundation—a distorted view of who Christ is, why he came to earth, and what the Bible and truth really are. And that has completely falsified the intent and purpose of Christianity. They read from the same Bible, talk of a personal relationship with God, and say biblical truth is important to their lives, but their beliefs and behavior are not consistent with what the Bible identifies as a true follower of Christ. We need to help our young people rebuild their faith and relationships with spiritual mentors from the ground up based on the true foundation of Christ.

Some time ago, a youth worker shared his struggle this way:

> I have ministered to my kids every week for a year now, and I've come to this conclusion: we use the same words as our young people, but they mean totally different things. Words like truth, tolerance, respect, acceptance, moral judgments, sin, the Holy Spirit, the devil, and redemption have a completely different meaning to my kids than they do to me. We were working from two different premises, and I didn't even know it. I'm con-

vinced unless I can get my kids to rethink these most basic Christian concepts, I'll never make it to square one with them.

This youth worker is confronting what every church and family confronts on a daily basis. Like him, many are unaware of the differing definitions their kids apply to words and the false concepts these definitions lead them to adopt. Notice just a few words in the following chart that mean different things to this emerging generation.

Word	Your Understanding (Adult Culture)	Postmodern Understanding (Youth Culture)
Tolerance	Accepting others without agreeing with or sharing their beliefs or lifestyle choices.	Accepting that each individual's beliefs, values, lifestyles, and truth claims are equal.
Respect	Giving due consideration to others beliefs and lifestyle choices without necessarily approving them.	Wholeheartedly approving of others' beliefs or lifestyle choices.
Acceptance	Embracing people for who they are, not necessarily for what they say or do.	Endorsing and even praising others for their beliefs and lifestyle choices.
Moral Judgments	Certain things are morally right and wrong as determined by God.	We have no right to judge another person's view or behavior.

Word	Your Understanding (Adult Culture)	Postmodern Understanding (Youth Culture)
Personal Preference	Preferences of color, food, clothing style, hobbies, etc., are personally determined.	Preferences of sexual behaviors, value systems, and beliefs are personally determined.
Personal Rights	Everyone has the right to be treated justly under the law.	Everyone has the right to do what he or she believes is best for himself or herself.
Freedom	Being free to do what you know you ought to do.	Being able to do anything you want to do.
Truth	An absolute standard of right and wrong.	Whatever is right for you.

These differences in meaning are symptomatic of a deeper problem—that the majority of our young people are neither understanding the claims of Christ nor becoming a true follower of him. And if we expect to make it to square one with this generation, we must correct the false concepts that our young people have about the entire Christian faith. Accomplish that and we have a chance to reintroduce the real and relevant Christ to our young people and witness a spiritual revolution of an entire generation.

Picture right now your son or daughter or the group of young people you love and care about. Now think twelve to fifteen years into the future and see them in their mid to late twenties. Imagine them being deeply devoted to Christ and passionately loving God with all their heart, mind, and strength. They know who they are as individuals, they know their strengths and weaknesses, and they are capitalizing on those strengths and compensating for their weaknesses. Consequently, they are highly valued and productive people.

Additionally, they have a great sense of purpose and direction in life: they know why they are here. Their life's goal is to honor and glorify their God by being devoted husbands or wives, loving fathers or mothers, faithful members of a local church and compassionate citizens of the world. They don't just talk about how culture needs to change; they are active participants in that change. Their neighbors are attracted to them because they demonstrate such a caring and compassionate heart by bringing healing to the hurting, comfort to the broken hearted, and help for those in need.

These young adults have a perspective on life and death that doesn't put a high premium on making lots of money or establishing a life of leisure and pleasure for themselves and their families. They sacrifice financially and give of themselves freely. Their eyes are not on this earthly kingdom but rather on a heavenly kingdom. Subsequently, they see themselves as pilgrims on a journey to a place not of this world, and they are intent on taking as many with them as they can.

Christianity to these godly men and women is far more than a system they have been taught or just believe—it is the life they live out every day. And what's more, they are instilling a Christlike way of life into their own children.

Is this the future you desire for your children and young people? Does this sound too good to actually come true—a hope and dream but not a realistic expectation? Well, it can be realistic if we as a collective body determine by God's grace to understand how to break through the distortions our young people have about Christianity and rebuild their faulty faith on the true foundations of Christ. I fear that if we don't, you and I might just be among the last Christian generation.

But there is still hope, and that is what this book is about—rebuilding the crumbling foundations of the true faith to raise up a new generation of Christ followers like that depicted in the above paragraphs. We will not attempt to identify all the "how to's" of the rebuilding process. Rather, we will lay out a "blueprint" of sorts—a clear picture enabling you to:

- **Understand the Distortions That Our Young People Have Adopted**

By realizing the extent to which our kids misunderstand Christianity, truth, reality, and the church, we gain a clearer understanding of both why and how we must lead them to become true followers of Christ.

- **Re-introduce God to Our Young People for who He Really Is**

Our kids don't truly understand God for who he really is. They must come to see the true God as a loving, relational being who came to reclaim them and restore all things to his original design.

- **Lead Our Young People to Properly Respond to God through a Spiritual Formation Process**

Being a true follower of Christ involves being conformed to the character of Christ. This involves very basic responses that our kids need to understand and make part of their everyday lives. We will identify seven such spiritual formation responses.

Much of my ministry has been to the youth culture, researching their thinking, identifying the top priorities facing them, speaking to those priorities, and creating resources to help families raise up children to be faithful followers of Christ. But neither my associates nor I work in a vacuum. We work closely with those ministering on the front lines of battle. In every youth issue we have addressed over the last thirty or so years, we have first called denominational and parachurch youth leaders together for a meeting. We ask them what youth issues are of highest priority and in what area they need the most help. They consistently ask for help in two areas. The first is printed and mediated resources that they can use to define the issues for their people and offer "how to" curriculum to help apply a solution. The second is effective "live" events and seminars presenting compelling content that will hold the attention of both parents and young people.

We have collaborated with those who are ministering effectively to parents and young people and drawn from the best of their working models. When we complete a resource for youth groups, we field test it with up to twenty-five youth groups before it is released. We do this to insure that the model can be replicated among even the smallest of youth groups.

What we are presenting in this book is no different. The crises we cite in these pages are from extensive research and interaction with church leaders and their youth. The biblical blueprint we offer here has come from three years of collaborating with local churches, denominational leaders, and parachurch groups. It is forged out of the experience of those with effective working models of ministry.

Our desire is to act as a catalyst and serve churches and families with a tried and proven message. And to that end, we pray that what is offered here will help you bring your young people to a face-to-face encounter with the one true God—the God who wants them to enjoy an intimate relationship with him, a relationship that will transform them into blameless and pure "children of God without fault in a crooked and depraved generation, in which [they] shine like stars in the universe" (Philippians 2:15, NIV).

Responding or Reacting?

Throughout history, Christian movements have responded to changing world cultures that have been detrimental to the social and spiritual development of our young people. These movements have helped to shape the church's view on many issues, including what is foundational to true Christianity. Such movements are often a response to, and sometimes even a reaction to, what is happening in the culture. And when we react, there is always the danger of swinging the pendulum too far in one way or the other.

It is apparent that here at the beginning of the twenty-first century we face a generation of young people who no longer hold to what most evangelicals consider to be the true foundations of the Christian faith: belief in the deity of Christ, the reliability of Scripture, and the bodily resurrection of Jesus. Whatever adjustments we make in the way we present the gospel to young people influenced by cultural thinking, those three pillars of the faith are central, crucial, and indispensable. And they are more than mere historical facts; they are crucially relevant to a person's everyday Christian life and relationships. We can and need to adjust the way we speak to today's culture, but we cannot budge one millimeter in our insistence that these pillars are absolutely essential to understanding not just our religion, but the entire structure of reality itself.

I spent years documenting the evidences for our faith, convinced that doing so would strengthen and deepen a believer's faith in God and his Word. But I must admit I was taken aback when I first learned that some churched young people didn't see the value in discovering the evidence for Christ's deity, his resurrection, or for the reliability of Scripture. It forced me and many Christian leaders to re-examine how we were presenting the Christian faith to this generation. Out of that re-examination comes this biblical blueprint to rebuild the true foundations of the Christian faith. What we will be presenting here may seem radical to some. And in a sense it is. It is nothing less than a call to a significant realignment, but it is by no means a new theology. It is based firmly upon sound biblical teaching.

What we are calling for is a resurgence of a Christ-centered, God-focused message that is biblical yet real and relevant to today's youth. We do not wish to merely make another defense for Christian evidences or a cognitive, intellectual approach to Christianity, and neither do we simply want to emphasize a warm, fuzzy relational heart message of Christianity. A reaction leading to either extreme can cause more damage than good.

We are calling for a spiritual revolution—a passionate embracing of the Christian faith for what it is—a vibrant relationship with the real and living person of Jesus Christ, to be lived out with our whole heart, mind, soul, and strength.

If we as churches and families keep doing what we're doing, we'll keep getting what we've got. And that is clearly not what we want. I've had some people tell me we simply need better church attendance and more sermons. That solution is like a sales manager's response to the accountant who told him that the company was losing ten dollars on every sale. "Then we'll just double our sales," said the sales manager. Doing more of what we're doing will not salvage this generation.

This is a call to correct the current distortion of Christianity among our young people without being alarmist or reactionary. We as a ministry have been asked by numerous denominations to help create a Christian catechism, if you will, that churches and families can adopt as a training tool. But these denominations and groups have stipulated that it not be simply another program. Because going through programs doesn't accomplish much unless a person learns to live out a Christlike life everyday. In that respect, the "program" we will be discussing throughout these pages isn't so much a program as it is a process—a way of coming to know God for who he is and responding to him by living and being a true follower of Christ.

Moving away from programs for programs' sake and adopting a process-driven model will be a challenge for many because it will require the abandonment of what some consider sacred—the "Structural Church" that is primarily concerned with conducting events to a spectator audience. Instead, we will encourage the embracing of a "Missional Church" that is focused on re-establishing a process of becoming more and more like Christ. This book will attempt to provide a clear, urgent, yet balanced biblical blueprint that may rattle many people's concept of Christianity, truth, and the church. We will in affect be offering a fresh model of how to minister to our children and young people.

So we pray that you find in the following pages a blueprint that is biblically founded, culturally relevant, and applicable to your ministry in doing your part to assure that you are not among the last Christian generation.

A Generation's Distorted Views

TWO
Our Young People's Distorted View of Christianity

"Goodbye, Endira," Melanie called from her door as her dark skinned friend walked to her car. She closed the door and went to the kitchen where her mother was preparing dinner.

"Endira seems like a very nice girl," said Melanie's mother as she took a bowl from the microwave. "She's quite mannerly and polite. I was wondering about the little dark spot on her forehead. Isn't that some religious mark?"

"Yes," replied Melanie, "She's Hindu. Her family is from India."

"What an opportunity for you!" her mother responded. "Since the two of you are becoming such good friends, you can be a Christian witness to her."

"I don't think so, Mom. You see, she—"

"What do you mean, 'you don't think so'? Surely with as much time as you spend with Endira, you wouldn't hesitate to let her know you're a Christian."

"Well, Mom, that's just the problem," replied Melanie as she began to set the table. "Endira believes that her religion is right for her, and I don't need to tell her otherwise. Because really, when you get right down to it, who's to say?"

"Who's to say!" Melanie's mother set the roast on the table and looked at her daughter. "God's to say, that's who. Surely you don't believe that Hinduism could possibly be true."

"The point is that Endira believes it to be true," replied Melanie. "And I just don't think I have the right to tell her she is wrong."

Why is it that the vast majority of our own churched kids (65%) either believes or suspects that there is "no way to tell which religion is true"?[1] Because your kids and mine have been influenced to believe that Christianity can't be exclusively true. You see, in your young people's minds, no one has the right to assert that one religion is better than another. They are taught (and have adopted) the creed of the culture that says all beliefs are equal. Recently, *Newsweek* and *Beliefnet* asked 1,004 Americans this question: "Can a good person who doesn't share your religious beliefs attain salvation or go to heaven?" Sixty-eight percent (68%) of evangelical protestants said yes.[2] The thinking is: "It's judgmental and intolerant to say that one person is right and everyone who doesn't believe like him or her is wrong." That's why sixty-three percent (63%) of our kids don't believe Jesus is the Son of the one true God. That seems to them too exclusive and intolerant. To them, Jesus is a son of God, but they can't bring themselves to say he is exclusively the Son of God.

It would be hard to argue against their viewpoint if Christianity was merely a system of beliefs as they have been led to believe. If Christianity was based solely on ethical teachings or theological concepts, then they'd be right—it would be one competing religion among many from which to choose. Sure, one could argue that the teachings of the Christian religion are better than other religious teachings, yet that would be a discussion about the superiority of one concept over another.

But Christianity isn't a mere religion, and it is not simply based upon various teachings. Christianity is based on the life, character, and identity of a person—Jesus Christ. Christ did not come to earth to teach Christianity—Christ *is* Christianity. That is what makes Christianity unique. It is a personal relationship with the personal creator God. Most religions of the world are based on philosophical propositions or theological ideologies. Remove its founding prophet or guru and that religion remains essentially intact. That is because these religions are based on the teachings, not upon the founding teacher.

That is not true of Christianity. While the Christian faith has a particular belief system and people have developed a theological construct from Scripture, its essential basis is the life, work, and person of its founder—Jesus Christ. This unique fact fundamentally changes the discussion. Instead of comparing the teachings of one religion to another, the essential question in Christianity is how a man or woman relates to the person of Jesus Christ. Remove Christ from Christianity, and you lose the entire meaning of biblical faith. As the apostle Paul said, if Christ isn't who he claimed to be and if he did not rise from the dead, then "our message has no meaning and your faith also has no meaning" (1 Corinthians 15:14, GWT).

This is why Jesus made himself the central issue. He said to the Pharisees, "Unless you believe that I am who I say I am, you will die in your sins" (John 8:24, NLT). The apostle John declared, "Life itself was in him, and this life gives light to everyone" (John 1:4, NLT). So while Jesus' teachings are important, they are important because of who he is and how they help us to relate properly to him.

Jesus' prayer to his Father defines the very essence of Christianity: "This is eternal life: to know you, the only true God, and Jesus Christ whom you sent" (John 17:3, GWT). Knowing God through Christ—having an intimate father-to-child relationship with him—is the essence of Christianity. Each of us and our children were born alienated from God because of sin. Sin is what separates us from God, yet God himself went to extraordinary lengths to cancel out our sin and bring us into an intimate father/child relationship with him. If it weren't for Christ, we could never become a child of God.

After coming to grips with the reality that Christianity is about Christ and how we are to become like him, a young man shared this with me:

> I used to engage in discussions with people on how certain things were right or wrong based on the teachings of the Bible. But the argument always ended up debating whose truth was true. Now, I point people to Christ as the person who defines the truth. The

discussion then centers on the claims Jesus made about himself and our need for a relationship with him.

This young man got it straight. The teachings from the Bible are not true because the theological concepts are superior to other religions; the teachings are true because they come from Christ, the true teacher.

Christianity isn't about Christ coming to earth to teach bad people how to live better as sixty-four percent (64%) of our young people believe.[3] Christianity is about Christ coming to earth to raise dead people to new life through a relationship with him! Jesus made it crystal clear to Saul (later Paul) on the road to Damascus that the focus is on how we all relate to Christ. Notice the emphasis Jesus makes when he reveals that Saul's destiny will be to share the gospel to the world: "You will open their eyes and turn them from darkness to light and from Satan's control to God's. Then they will receive forgiveness for their sins and a share among God's people who are made holy by believing in me" (Acts 26:18, emphasis mine, GWT).

How are we made holy and acceptable to God? The majority of our churched young people say they become acceptable to God by "doing enough good things for others during their life."[4] Their brand of Christianity is focused on earning an eternal standing with God. Jesus declared, on the other hand, that forgiveness of sin was absolutely necessary in order to become a relational child of God who is "made holy by *believing in me*."

When we fail to put a proper focus on Christ as the centerpiece for reclaiming his children back in relationship with God, it diminishes in the minds of our young people the importance of who Christ is and what he did for us. When we fail to keep Christ the central issue, Christianity becomes simply one religious truth among other religious truths. It also leads our young people to ignore key players such as Satan as the archenemy of God (65% of our kids don't believe Satan is real). And it explains why the majority (68%) of our kids don't consider the Holy Spirit as God's transforming agent and the empowerment for Christlike living but rather as just an influence for good. When we fail to emphasize Christ and our relationship with him as the centerpiece of Christianity, the entire foundation of Christianity crumbles.

How could this have happened? How can a generation raised largely in the church and from good Christian homes so misunderstand the essence of Christianity? It is not surprising when you realize that the majority of our young people have not been systematically and sufficiently indoctrinated into the true faith. Instead, they have been indoctrinated by a culture that places a premium on all religious beliefs being equal.

The Effects of the Distortion

The implications of our young people's distorted view of Christianity are far reaching. Most are trying to earn their way to heaven. That doesn't mean they have rejected Christ; they haven't. Many personally believe Jesus is their way to God, and if they follow his teachings and do enough good in life, they believe they're home free. But their lives are treadmills of performance. To them, good performance equals acceptance. The culture around them reinforces it at school, in sports, with friends, and even at home. They may pray "the Sinner's Prayer," but to their ears, it sounds like: "God, I'm sorry for all the bad I've done and I promise to do better. I really will. Amen."

While our young people may not state it like this, they have adopted the salvation equation: "When I perform, I'll be transformed." It's no wonder that the majority of our kids who profess Christianity struggle to live Christ-like lives. Because we are not transformed as a result of doing good things. We can try to live better in our own strength, but that does not produce the transformation God requires. Transformation is a supernatural experience resulting from God as our redeemer responding to us crying out in faith:

> I want to know you, O God, but I'm hopelessly
> lost in sin and in need of your forgiveness. I
> place my trust in the sacrificial death of your
> Son who nailed my sins to his cross. Forgive
> me and transform me from the inside out—
> from a person dead in sin into a new person
> alive in intimate relationship with you!

When our young people understand and yield to this truth, a mysterious and miraculous change takes place. You don't earn it. You don't deserve it. You can't buy it. You simply receive the person of truth into your life by the grace of the "God who is passionate about his relationship with you" (Exodus 34:14, NLT). That is the God our young people need to clearly see and that is the faith response they need to be led to make. That is at the very foundation of what Christianity is all about, and unless we rebuild that most basic truth within the church and our church families, how will our young people ever come to know the true God?

To make matters worse, our young people not only have a distorted view of what Christianity is but also a distorted view of what truth is and how we are to relate to it. And it's actually their perception of truth that spiritually cripples them from both seeing the true God and responding to his transforming power.

THREE
Our Young People's Distorted View of Truth

I was speaking at a denominational youth conference attended by the best kids this large denomination had to offer. They were the cream of the crop—solid Christian kids. Because I was planning to talk the next day about the truth of the Bible, I went from one person to another in the course of my address and asked, "Why do you believe the Bible to be true?"

Not one kid had an answer. One after another tried, but none came up with a credible response.

The next morning, a young man ran up to me and shouted, "Josh, I know the answer!"

He caught me off-guard. "The answer to what?" I asked.

"To your question about why I believe the Bible is true."

"Okay," I said, "let's hear it."

"Because I believe," he answered emphatically. "Because I have faith."

"You're saying it's true because you believe it?" I asked.

"Yes!" He couldn't have sounded more convinced.

I looked around at the youth directors and kids who had gathered to listen. Many of them smiled and nodded their heads as though this young man had solved a great riddle, and it now all seemed so obvious.

I then asked him, "Does this mean it would make the Bible true for your friends at school?"

"It would be if they believed it," he said.

I gazed at him for a few seconds. His answers saddened me deeply, but I knew he was all too typical of our kids today. Finally, I said, "You know the basic difference between you and me?"

"What?" he asked.

"To you," I said, "the Bible is true because you believe it. To me, I believe it because it's true."

Alarming as it may be, the majority of our young people today—even the brightest and best of them—are in agreement with that young man. They have adopted the view that moral truth is not true for them *until they choose to believe it*. They believe that *the act of believing makes things true*. And then, once they believe, those things will be true for them *only until they choose to believe something else*. As soon as something more appealing comes along, they are likely to begin believing *that*—whether or not it's biblical.

Permeating Our Society

We're not suggesting that the church or Christian families have intentionally instilled the view that all moral truth is only truth when you choose to believe it. What has happened is this: In the absence of foundational training, our young people have been influenced by a philosophy that permeates much of our society—government, schools, movies, television, and music—and guides much of their behaviors without them (or most of us) even being aware of it. This extremely complex, often contradictory, and constantly changing school of thought can be summarized as the postmodern belief that:

- Moral and religious truth does not exist in any objective sense.

- Instead of "discovering" truth in a story (such as the Bible) that presents a unified way of looking at life—postmodernism rejects any overarching explanation of what constitutes truth and reality.

- Truth—whether in science, education, or religion—is created by a specific culture or community and is "true" only in and for that culture.

- Individual persons are the product of their cultures. That is, we are not essentially unique individuals created in the image of God; our identities are defined by our culture (African-American, European, Eastern, Western, urban, rural, etc.).

- All thinking is a "social construct." In other words, what you and I regard as truths are simply arbitrary "beliefs we have been conditioned to accept by our society, just as others have been conditioned to accept a completely different set of beliefs."[1]

- Any system or statement that claims to be objectively true or unfavorably judges the values, beliefs, lifestyle, and truth claims of another culture is a power play, an effort by one culture to dominate other cultures.

Our young people, along with the culture at large, have not so much consciously adopted these concepts of truth as much as they have absorbed them over time. This cultural mindset has permeated every level of today's society.

No Universal Truth

A few years ago, tens of thousands of high school young people took a pledge to be sexually pure until marriage. These kids participated in the "True Love Waits" campaign and took a stand for the truth on sexual purity. That certainly was an encouraging stance in the midst of a promiscuous society. The problem, however, was that most young people heard that truth through their own "filter," which told them that all truth is subjectively determined. In other words, premarital sex was wrong only if they personally believed it was wrong.

Imagine my conversation with a fifteen-year-old Christian young lady. Let's call her Chrissy. I've had many such conversations with young people with precisely this outcome.

"Is premarital sex wrong?" I ask.
"Well, I believe it's wrong for me," she replies.

> "But," I continue, "do you believe sex before marriage is wrong for everyone?"
> Chrissy begins to squirm, visibly uncomfortable, as she answers.
> "Well, I just believe it's wrong for me and I'm waiting until marriage. But I can't judge what other people believe and do."

Chrissy and the majority of our young people (81%) have adopted a view that "all truth is relative to the individual and his/her circumstances."[2] So while our kids may be willing to state that certain things are right or wrong, they believe that it applies only to them personally. It's not surprising then that seventy percent (70%) of our churched young people believe there is no absolute moral truth.[3] In other words, the vast majority of young people from good churches and homes do not believe there is a truth outside themselves that determines right from wrong. They do not believe there is a universal truth that is right for all people, in all places, at all times. They have been conditioned to believe that each individual has been given the right to say and do what that person thinks is best for him or her.

This approach appeals to our kids' desire to be themselves, to be free, and to be autonomous. It appeals to their desire to respect others' choices and to refrain from judging other people's decisions. And since our kids believe many ways are right, they believe they have to create the way that is best for them. They see truth in the area of religion and morality as a personal and private matter, and they surmise that no one should be allowed to impose his or her own ideas of what is right or wrong on another.

So when we share a scriptural truth, whether that be from the Ten Commandments or the truth of Christ's resurrection, our kids will tend to see it as something they might believe subjectively for themselves, but they do not necessarily consider it to be an objective truth.

My son Sean McDowell once performed the following experiment to help a group of Christian high school students grasp the reality of Jesus' resurrection as objectively true. He set up his experiment and related it this way:

> I placed a jar of marbles in front of them and asked, "How many marbles are in the jar?" They responded with different guesses, 221, 168, 149, and so on. Then after giving them the correct number of 188, I asked, "Which of you is closest to being right?" They all agreed that 168 was the closest guess. And they all agreed that the number of marbles was a matter of fact, not personal preference.
>
> Then I passed out *Starburst* candies to each one of my students and asked, "Which flavor is right?" As you might expect, they all felt this was an unfair question because each person had a preference that was right for him or her. "That is correct," I concluded, "the right flavor has to do with a person's preferences. It is a matter of subjective opinion, not objective fact."
>
> Then I asked, "Is the resurrection of Jesus like the number of marbles in a jar, or is it a matter of personal opinion, like candy preference?" Most of my students concluded that the question of the resurrection belonged

in the category of candy preference. I concluded the experiment by talking about the nature of Jesus' physical resurrection—that if we were present at the cross we could have felt the warm blood of Jesus trickling down the wooden planks or even watched him take his last breath. And if we were at the tomb on that morning, we would have seen the stone rolled away and the loincloth of Jesus sitting inside. I reminded them that while many people may reject the historical resurrection of Jesus, it is not the type of claim that can be "true for you, but not true for me." The tomb was either empty on the third day, or it was occupied—there is no middle ground.

The problem is that our young people are applying to all questions a mode of thinking that is legitimate only for certain types of questions. While tastes in candy are certainly a matter of personal preference, that does not mean that questions about truth can be determined in the same way. Truth is either objectively true and conforms to reality, or it is simply not truth. Personal preference does not affect the question at all. The attempt to determine spiritual and moral truth by personal preference will lead to certain disaster as it did in ancient Israel in the time when "everyone did whatever he considered right" (Judges 17:6, GWT). The resulting anarchy led to unprecedented depravity and the near annihilation of one tribe. Treating universal truth as personal preference is disastrous because God never intended us to see scriptural truth as optional or to position ourselves as the sole arbiters of what is right or wrong. But that is precisely what our young people are doing, and consequently, they are making wrong choices...while thinking they are right.

Earlier we quoted statistics showing the number of professed Christian young people who lie, cheat, hurt one another, and so on. Unfortunately, this isn't a matter of churched kids doing these things out of weakness or in spite of their standards and later confessing they're wrong. This is a generation that is doing these things from their "personal standard of morality" and justifying them as acceptable under the circumstances. In other words, our young people have a distorted view of what makes things right and wrong. They have lost the universal standard for what is moral and ethical, and the result is a culture of young people vulnerable not only to wrong thinking but also to the destructive consequences of wrong behavior.

The need has never been more urgent. We must (in Paul's words) equip this next generation with the truth and help them to grow "in [the] knowledge about God's Son, until [they] become mature, until [they] measure up to Christ, who is the standard. Then [they] will no longer be like little children, tossed and carried about by all kinds of teachings that change like the wind" (Ephesians 4:14, GWT).

Unless we restore Christ—not their own opinions and choices—to his rightful place as *the* standard, our kids won't have a chance. We must reintroduce Christ to our kids until they see him as the person of truth that wants a personal relationship with them. And we must lead them to respond to him as a hurting child would respond to the loving arms of a mother or father. When our young people are grounded in a love relationship with Christ, they will no longer be "tossed and carried about" by all kinds of destructive forces that abound in the culture around them. Rather, they will become grounded in the truth of scripture and see reality as God sees it. But the problem is, our young people don't see from God's perspective, and they have a distorted view of reality. We'll take that up in the next chapter.

FOUR
Our Young People's Distorted View of Reality

It's an experiment you probably first performed in grade school. It begins with a clear glass and a spoon. You fill the glass two-thirds full of water and place the spoon in the glass. Instantly, the handle of the spoon appears broken where it enters the water and bent when viewed from another angle. However, when you lift the spoon out of the glass, it is still straight and in one piece.

In reality, the spoon was never bent; the light was. It's called refraction, the bending of light as it passes between materials of different density (in this case air and water). That phenomenon causes the observer to see a distorted view of reality, seeing as crooked something that is in fact straight.

That aptly depicts the situation in which we find our kids today. They are as bright as any generation before them—if not brighter. They are promising. They are perceptive…but unfortunately, their perception of reality is dangerously distorted. And, as a result, even the most committed among them is ill-equipped to distinguish straight from crooked, right from wrong, and wisdom from foolishness.

The Way Things Work

A recent survey by the Online Computer Library Center revealed that David Macaulay's *The Way Things Work* was on more public library shelves in the United States than any other children's book.[1] That's understandable since today's young people may be the most pragmatic generation ever. They want what is real, relevant, and "right now." This generation, as a rule, is not asking "Is it true?" but rather "Does it work?" Along this line, author Rick Richardson (*Evangelism Outside the Box*) has said, "[They] have redefined truth as "whatever rings true to your experience, whatever *feels* real to you."[2]

If Hugh Hefner's motto, "If it feels good, do it," characterized the sixties, today's culture propagates the view that "if it works, it's right." That is, the test of whether an action is right or wrong is not based on some objective standard but simply upon the desirability of the outcome.

Of course, this is not a new philosophy. But what *is* new is the degree to which it is reflected in our children's thinking and acting. In fact, seventy-two percent (72%) of them believe that "you can tell if something is morally/ethically right for you by whether or not it works in your life."[3]

A Flawed Perspective

Our young people have bought into this way of processing and perceiving reality—a way that says "what works right now is right for now." Still, that perception, like the "broken" spoon in the glass, is an illusion. The Bible repeatedly makes it clear that the credo "If it works, it's right" does not reflect the way things really are.

When Joseph, the son of Jacob, was a slave in Egypt and was propositioned by his master's wife, he did not pause to ask himself, "Would this work for me?" Instead, the Bible records his response: "How could I do such a wicked thing and sin against God?" (Genesis 39:9, NIV).

When David, who had sinned with Bathsheba and then engineered the death of her husband, was confronted by Nathan the prophet, David did not say, "Nathan, it works just fine for me, so don't try to impose your morality on my behavior." On the contrary, once his action was exposed, David responded in no uncertain terms, "I have sinned against the Lord" (2 Samuel 12:13, GWT).

When Jesus, who was overburdened with the imminence of his execution, cried out to his Father in the garden of Gethsemane, he did not protest, "This isn't working for me!" No, instead he said, "Father, if it is your will, take this cup of suffering away from me. However, your will must be done, not mine" (Luke 22:42, GWT).

The majority of today's young people make their decisions by the credo, "If it works, it's right." But God's perspective of reality says, "If it's right, it will work," for if you "Obey [God's] directions, laws, commands, rules and written instruction...then you'll succeed in everything you do wherever you may go" (1 Kings 2:3, GWT). Ours is a cause-and-effect world in which God communicated to us his ways, ways that are based on universal—not pragmatic—standards. His ways protect us from harm. His ways provide safety and blessing for us. But our kids don't see it that way. And their distorted perception of reality is not only flawed; it also leads to heartache and suffering.

A Dangerous Perspective

Remember the story of the pied piper? The German town of Hamelin engaged the boy with the magic melody to rid their town of rats, which he did. But once the rats were gone, the town's officials took a pragmatic approach: the rats were no longer a problem, and the solution had come about so easily that they saw no reason to pay the piper. Worked for them, right? Wrong. The piper came up with his own solution, one that worked for him. He played his pipe for the children of the town and enticed them all to the same fate the rats had met.

Similarly, such a distorted view of reality will lead our own children to destruction. Millard Erickson, professor of Theology at Truett University, writes:

> What is the time span for the evaluation of ideas? Is a true idea one which will work immediately? In a year from now? In ten years? In a hundred years?...Popular pragmatism tends to assume that immediate workability is the criterion. Yet what is expedient in the short term often turns out to be inexpedient in the long run.[4]

Our young people's distorted view of reality—of the way this cause-and-effect world really operates—will lead them down a path of destruction if that view is not corrected. If "immediate workability" is their criterion in making choices, they will be more readily induced into instant gratification, temporary fixes, and expedient answers that promise not the provision and protection of God's ways but deceit and destruction.

Rapper Lil' Kim lied to a federal grand jury about a shoot-out outside a New York City radio station. When she was later sentenced to prison for lying, she said, "At the time, I thought it was the right thing to do, but I now know it was wrong."[5] Did Lil' Kim think lying was right because it would keep her out of trouble and then decide it must be wrong when it landed her in prison? Our youth culture certainly does. They have adopted the view of "immediate workability." And with that criterion almost anything goes.

If "immediate workability" is our young people's criterion, then taking steroids to enhance athletic performance seems worth doing. If "immediate workability" is their criterion, premarital sex will seem like a viable option. If "immediate workability" is their criterion, cheating may promise easier and more desirable results than studying. Lying like that of the rapper will often appear to be a much more workable solution than facing the sometimes uncomfortable consequences of telling the truth.

Not only that, but if "immediate workability" is their criterion, who among them will choose sacrifice over selfishness? Who will choose the cross instead of the culture? Who will choose righteousness rather than self-gratification? If our youth are not helped to see reality from God's perspective, how will they respond to the call of God, to his will, or to his desires for them?

That is why we desperately need to move our young people from the distorted and faulty premise upon which they make choices and help them see God for who he is and how he relates to them. Then they will be able to distinguish right from wrong, truth from error, and good from bad. We must help them to understand that Scripture is a revelation of the living God who wants them to know him for who he is and respond by entrusting their futures to his sovereign will. Our young people need a spiritual experience that will transform their pragmatic mindset into such a passionate relationship with God that they readily respond to Jesus' admonition to "love the Lord your God with all your heart, with all your soul, and with all your mind. This is the greatest and most important commandment. The second is like it: Love your neighbor as you love yourself" (Matthew 22:37–39, GWT).

FIVE
Our Young People's Distorted View of the True Church

"Perception is reality." You have probably heard the saying. Perhaps you've even used it. The point of the expression is that what people perceive to be true may as well be true. For example, if investors perceive a company to be a great value, it may, in fact, turn out to be a good value as more and more people buy it.

But, of course, there is a problem with such thinking. Despite the perceptions of investors, the energy giant Enron was not a wise investment in the 1990's, and perception did not prevent the eventual collapse of the company. Similarly, most of our young people perceive the church today in a particular way, but their perception is a distortion of what the true church is…and sadly many churches are a distortion of what God wants them to be.

After examining the research on today's youth and reflecting on my own interaction with thousands of young people, I can paint you a fair picture of the view most teenagers have of the church—defined primarily by their experience of the church's youth ministry or youth group. While these perceptions may accurately reflect their experience and perception, they are not accurate reflections of what the church was meant to be. And while studies reveal that today's young people are actually more active in church-sponsored events and faith practices than adults, their views of the church give us reason to believe it's time for wholesale changes in the way youth ministry is done.[1] Here is what church looks like to them:

1. CHURCH IS BORING

Kids go to youth group primarily for the fun, food, and fellowship they can get out of it. But to most, the youth leader's "spiritual devotional" is boring. Keep in mind that over half of today's churches are less than seventy-five in attendance, and only the top ten percent of churches can afford a full-time youth leader. So youth group for most kids involves a small number of students led by a volunteer youth worker with little expertise and little time to prepare. And it shows. What most kids do is endure the devotion time to enjoy the food, fellowship, and fun of hanging out with friends afterward. Typically, these fellowship times have little spiritual content and may differ only slightly from their association with kids at school or other places.

2. CHURCH IS NON-STOP ACTIVITY

On the surface, this may seem like a contradiction to the view that church is boring, but young people who attend a large youth group with a full-time youth minister will often say, "Group is a blast." The traditional approach of many full-time youth ministers is entertainment, entertainment, entertainment.

Many people involved in youth ministry believe that the rise of electronic media—television, movies, video games, computer games and online services—have made "stimulation addicts" of many teens and have adversely affected their attention spans. Movies and television change images every couple of seconds, and kids' minds get used to that. As a result, they, at times, find it difficult to focus on any form of content for any extended period of time.

Consequently, youth group meetings are often filled with high-energy games, interactive participation, trips, retreats, and all the entertainment imaginable, plus a few minutes of devotions. To our kids, the churchy part of church may be boring, but the frenzy of activity that youth pastors generate to keep them involved with church keeps them going, and going, and going. But the question is, "going where?"

3. CHURCH ISN'T THE BIGGEST INFLUENCE IN MY LIFE OR MY SPIRITUAL DEVELOPMENT

How would the typical churched young person answer this question: "As a teenager, who or what is molding and shaping your attitudes and actions?" Seventy-eight percent (78%) of them say: "It's my parents." Studies show that their parents have three times the influence over them than their pastor or youth group leader. Church is seventh on their list, carrying just as much influence as does their music. In fact, their friends have twice as much influence over them than their youth group leader."[2]

The prevalent idea that movies and TV have the greatest influence on our kids' lives simply doesn't hold up under the research. It may feel better to identify Hollywood, MTV, and today's culture as the main source of our problem, but the fact remains that we as parents have the greatest influence and opportunity to instill our values and faith within our children. Sure, the culture is a powerful enemy and has had a devastating influence on our young people, and it is true that this influence has distorted their perception of Christianity, truth, and reality. But would our young people be where they are today if parents and the church were models of Christlikeness relationally connecting with their kids, engaging in a concerted effort to reveal who God really is, and leading them to respond as a true follower of Christ?

We are not saying that we shouldn't take a stand against profanity, sex, and violence on TV and in movies and video games, but parents have six times more influence over teenagers than TV does and almost eight times more influence than movies.[3] Parents, therefore, carry far more weight—for good or bad—than they give themselves credit for. How a child thinks and acts is still molded by his or her home life, which means the crumbling foundations of the faith among this generation is as much a parental problem as a church problem, if not more so. If we're going to reclaim the next generation, then the home and the church must join forces together like never before.

4. CHURCH SEEMS LIKE JUST A SERIES OF EVENTS TO ME

To most of our young people (and even many adults) church is more like a tennis match than a block party. That is, many churches look to them more like an observing and listening place than a participating and interacting community. Worship music often invites participation, of course, but beyond that, there is little room in many churches for interactive, relational discovery of the truth.

Teenagers today are perhaps the most relational and community-oriented generation in history. And most church events simply don't engage young people and adults in a relational interaction about the truth of God's Word. In other words, they don't interact together on how the truth is to be lived out within relationships.

Studies on today's youth reveal that relationships score extremely high in the hearts and minds of our young people.[4] Your own observations probably confirm that conclusion. Young people rank "close, personal friendships," "one marriage partner for life," "a close relationship with God," and "influencing other people's lives" so highly that Barna says, "One of the distinguishing marks of [today's kids] has been their insistence upon the importance of personal relationship...[They] appear to esteem relationships more highly than has been the norm for more than a quarter century."[5] Spectator events have their place, but when it comes to a relational, community-minded, interactive generation, mere church events don't cut it.

5. CHURCH MAY HELP SAVE MY SOUL BUT IT WON'T HELP ME GRAPPLE WITH THE REAL ISSUES OF MY LIFE

Before Rick Warren started Saddleback Community Church in California, he set out to determine why people didn't attend church and what advice they had for a church that wanted to help others. The number one complaint he heard was that to most people "church is boring, especially the sermons. The messages don't relate to my life."[6] It is no different with today's young people.

The research tells us that kids know the church cares about saving their soul. In fact, if they haven't trusted Christ for salvation prior to age thirteen, they probably never will.[7] But what about the rest of their life? They need a process we can take them through to help them figure out the purpose and meaning of life. Seventy-four percent (74%) of all teenagers admit that they don't have life figured out.[8] Sixty-three percent (63%) say that they don't have any comprehensive and clear philosophy about life that consistently influences their lifestyle and decisions.[9]

George Barna laid it out in no uncertain terms when he said our young people come to youth group...

> Because their friends are there and believe the church has the potential to deliver useful insights. If they are not allowed to bond with their friends while at the church they probably will not return. Similarly, if the church provides the trappings of substance (hot music, casual and friendly ambiance, fun activities) but not the substance, they are not likely to return. The substance must be de-

livered with relevance—modern, practical, contextualized. Anything less than a marriage of style and substance is tantamount to walking them to the door and asking them to depart.[10]

The sad reality is that they are departing. Yes, we want to keep our young people engaged in church, but if we don't offer a relevant message, most will not stay. And, as we've said, if we keep doing what we're doing, we'll keep getting what we've got. Still, even in the midst of this gloomy picture, there is a ray of hope.

Why There is Hope

There is hope for our kids because of two of the statistics we quoted above: seventy-four percent (74%) of them still haven't figured out the purpose or meaning of their lives, and sixty-three percent (63%) do not have a comprehensive and clear "philosophy about life that consistently influences their lifestyle and decisions." That means every church and family has a golden opportunity. Our young people are in just the right place to grab hold of a discovery process that is real, relational, and relevant to everyday life.

Second, there is hope for our teens because it is clear that they are not rejecting God. They may not see God for who he is, and consequently, they may not be properly responding to him, but most of them are open and receptive to a true relationship with him.

Third, there is hope because God is still God, and his Spirit and his Word are still alive and relevant to this generation. God is still in the business of transforming men and women from a dead existence into a vital relationship with him.

And fourth, there is hope because there is a growing awareness among churches and families that we truly are losing the next generation. There is a rising sense of urgency in many churches and families along with an increasing willingness to do something about it.

We asked scores of Christian leaders to identify ten "life issues" that they considered critical if our kids are going to become healthy and mature relationally, morally, and spiritually. We then surveyed over two thousand youth workers to determine the importance of these issues in order of priority. Following are the top five chosen. They are an impressive set of priorities:

THE TOP 5 PRIORITY ISSUES

1. That my kids experience a transformed life in Christ (chosen by 84% of all surveyed).
2. That they know why they believe what they believe (chosen by 41% of all surveyed).
3. That they develop healthy relationships (chosen by 35% of all surveyed).
4. That they learn to resist ungodly influences (chosen by 23% of all surveyed).
5. That they discover how to make right choices (chosen by 18% of all surveyed).[11]

Then we asked over two thousand youth workers to identify the top five challenges facing them as they attempt to salvage this generation. In this case, we provided no list from which to choose, and yet the following challenges were overwhelmingly identified by most of the respondents:

THE TOP 5 CHALLENGES

1. Developing passionate followers of Christ.
2. Making Christ and Scripture real and relevant to kids.
3. Getting kids to know—and live—the truth.
4. Helping kids combat ungodly influences.
5. Ministering intergenerationally.[12]

The above priorities and challenges show that most youth workers know what needs to be done. Although this is encouraging, the pivotal question is: "What do we do about it?" To correct the distorted views that our young people have embraced and to see their lives truly transformed will require a fundamental change in the way most churches are doing ministry and most families are raising their young people. What we will propose here is not a more palatable gospel, but rather an "unsanitized gospel" that makes perfectly clear what it means to become a follower of Christ. What does that look like and what will it take to break through the distorted views of this generation?

THE LAST CHRISTIAN GENERATION

66

SIX
What Will It Take?

One of the many benefits of the internet is the proliferation of programs that aid the translation of words, phrases, and even whole documents from one language into another. These programs are already helping churches, businesses, and individuals break through language barriers. Nevertheless, translation software and websites have limitations. Trying to translate a phrase from English into another language and then back again into English to check the accuracy often yields surprising results.

For example, the meaning of the following common English terms, when translated by software programs into another language, often lose something to say the least. "All's well that ends well" translated into German becomes "all sleeve from that, which the ends spray out." "There's no time like the present" translated into Italian becomes "Before no more time it appreciate the gift." And "the best defense is a good offense" translated into Spanish becomes "the defense is a more better possible good action."

Our attempts to reach this generation with the gospel message of Christ can suffer from similar translation failures. In a sense, our young people speak another language. Yes, it's English, of course, and we all use the same words and phrases. But our kids don't always put the same meaning that we do to certain words and phrases, and they relate better to some modes of communication than to others. It is critical that we translate the gospel message using terms and modes of communication that this generation can understand without changing its true meaning. Our task is to translate the good news so that our kids recognize it as the relevant, life-changing message that it is. But that will require a change in our thinking.

Our first task in translating the gospel so that our young people will understand it is to become living models of it in our very lives. All of us—as individuals, as families, and as the Church—must move beyond mere proclamation (as necessary as that is) to a "lived-out gospel," whereby we model and demonstrate a transformed life of devotion to God and love of others to this generation. There is absolutely no substitute for this. No message will sink in faster or take root deeper than one that is demonstrated by the nature of our lives. We must show that it means something to us before we can expect it to mean anything to them.

This "lived-out gospel" is nothing new. It is no different from what the apostles and early church did and taught in the first century. "Therefore be imitators of God," Paul said, "as beloved children; and walk in love, just as Christ also loved you" (Ephesians 5:1-2, NASB). We simply need to reclaim that process that was once an intrinsic part of the gospel message. When we do, our kids will not only hear the truth proclaimed but will also see the transforming power of Christ in action in the lives of the parents, children's workers, teachers, and youth workers who minister to them. And then from that platform, they can be effectively led to experience Christ in their own lives as well.

The Need for a True Revelation

In previous chapters, we have described how the distortions of the Christian faith concerning truth and reality that our young people have adopted results in negative consequences. Sadly, the majority of our young people are not being transformed. They are making wrong choices and suffering the consequences, all the while believing they are Christians.

Still, the solution isn't in just telling them what a Christian does and doesn't do, as important as that is. I believe the solution lies **in revealing to this generation of young people who Christ really is and then leading them to properly respond to him.** Our young people's distorted views and unchanged lives will continue until they experience a true revelation of Christ for who he really is.

During World War II, men left their young families and were sometimes gone for years. Many small children grew up not knowing their fathers. Picture the scene of a four-year-old girl named Sarah whose daddy had been off to war for over two years. Little Sarah didn't remember her daddy, but her mother had been diligent about making his reality alive in her mind. She told her little girl how daddy still provided money for their house, clothes, and food. She read her his letters containing endearing expressions of love for his daughter. Those letters also asked Sarah to be brave while he was gone and to help mommy by hanging up her clothes and picking up her toys. He admonished her to be kind to the neighbor children when she played and to always say her prayers at night.

The mother spent time explaining to Sarah what her daddy was like—of his providing and protecting nature, his caring love, his honesty and integrity, his sense of honor and duty to family and country. She let her daughter know how deeply in love she was with Sarah's father. Sarah's mother guided her young daughter in knowing how to respond to such a loving father when he returned from the war.

Then one day, Sarah's mother announced that her father was coming home. The little girl was overjoyed. She couldn't wait to see in person the man she had only seen in pictures. And when she met him at the airport, she ran eagerly to his open arms. She responded with love to her father because she had been taught how to love him by someone who knew and loved him herself.

The responsibility of the church and families is to do as Sarah's mother did—reveal the true nature of God to our children and lead them to a proper response to him. None of us naturally knows how to respond properly to God. We need instruction and training. We even need instruction and training to know how to respond and relate to each other. Developing a healthy marriage is a learning process. Effective parenting is a learning process. And becoming a committed follower of Christ is no different; we need to learn and go through a growing process. We must reveal the true nature of God to our children and young people and then instruct them through a process of how to respond properly and relate to him. We all need to be discipled in Christ, and because our kids have distorted views of God and are building their faith and lives on a faulty foundation, we must lead them to rebuild on the true foundation. We do that by first modeling and then proclaiming the true revelation of God himself to this generation.

Three True Foundations of the Faith

There are three foundational characteristics of God that give us a true revelation of who he is. These characteristics are not necessarily all that God is, but they reveal the very essence of his heart. Each of these foundational characteristics, when understood in our hearts and minds, draws from us a specific response. Our response is all-important, for it actually opens the door for the empowering presence of Christ to transform us, give us purpose for living, and define our very mission in life. Yet our response to Christ is not a one-time event; it is a continual living and growing relational process—what we are calling the *spiritual formation process.* It is the process of developing the character of Christ in our lives. It is the process of becoming more and more like Christ under the loving direction of the Holy Spirit and the Word of God.

The foundations and the process work together in this way: First, we come to know God for who he is—to understand his very heart. Then our correct and clear understanding of who God is motivates us to respond to him in specific ways. This is not, as we said, a one-time response but rather an ongoing relational interaction with God that step-by-step conforms us to the image of Christ.

In this chapter, we will highlight the process of presenting a clear revelation of God and responding to him. Then, in subsequent chapters, we will deal more in depth with the particular facets of our response.

FOUNDATION #1: THE GOD OF REDEMPTION WHO GAVE HIS VERY LIFE

We've heard the words and phrases so much in church that we almost become immune to the incredible meaning of the fact: The God who created the universe came to earth to give his life to save us from being lost from him forever. It's a fact too astounding to grasp fully. But it's true—absolutely true. To know that God is the God of redemption gives us an insight into a God who accepts us unconditionally. Despite our sin, Christ died to reclaim us. Most of our kids have failed to grasp both the depth of our sin and depravity and God's marvelous love revealed in his redemptive heart. Uncovering the deep meaning of God's redemptive heart will open our young people's hearts and minds to a whole new understanding of who God truly is.

OUR RESPONSE TO
THE GOD OF REDEMPTION

What should our response be when we know that God accepted us so unconditionally that he came and died to redeem us even when we sinned against him? The apostle Paul tells us: "Brothers and sisters, because of God's compassion toward us, I encourage you to offer your bodies a living sacrifice, dedicated to God and pleasing to him" (Romans 12:1, GWT). The New Living Translation follows this with a question, "When you think of what he has done for you, is this too much to ask?" (Romans 12:16, NLT).

"Is this too much to ask?" he questions. Hardly! God sacrifices himself to save us and tells us that our proper response is to sacrifice ourselves. Jesus said, "If any of you wants to be my followers, you must put aside your selfish ambitions, shoulder your cross daily, and follow me. If you try to keep your life for yourself, you will lose it. But if you give up your life for me, you will find true life" (Luke 9:23–24, NLT). If we as a church and as families truly reveal the depths of God's redemptive heart to our children and young people, they will sense the call of Christ to give of themselves as a living sacrifice to God.

We are convinced that today's young people are ready to respond positively to a call for sacrifice. They have seen through the shallow values of easy believism and various attempts to cajole them by imitating the entertainment of the world, and as a result, that kind of Christianity looks meaningless to many of them. Our kids need substance from the church. They are turned off by false values and empty materialism. They are ready to give themselves to something—more accurately to give something of themselves to someone who has given his very life for them.

We can direct them toward three specific responses to the God who died to save them: the development of a life of **firm faith, devoted worship of God, and effectual prayer**. These three responses encompass the critical meaning of becoming a living sacrifice, and they are our only appropriate response to the redeemer who died for us. In chapter seven, we will explore them in detail.

FOUNDATION #2: THE GOD OF RELATIONSHIPS WHO GAVE HIS SPIRIT AND THE WORD

A fact every bit as astounding as God's dying for us is that he created us for relationship with him in the first place. It is critically important that we help our young people understand that he made us specifically for the purpose of living in joyful and intimate relationship with him. As hard as it is to fathom, the God of the universe delighted in his close companionship with Adam and Eve in the garden, and it was his intention to have that kind of relationship with every one of us. The reality that we must lead our kids to understand is that God responds to our faith, worship, and prayer in a very specific manner. Because he is the God of relationships, he gives us his Spirit and his Word that we might know him so intimately that he literally lives in and through our very lives. This intimate bonding with God's Word and his Holy Spirit with every believer is the foundation of our relationship with him. Revealing the riches of God's relational heart uncovers the very purpose for living. Our young people need to understand that the Word and the Holy Spirit are there to empower them to become more and more like Christ.

OUR RESPONSE TO THE GOD OF RELATIONSHIPS

When our young people understand that God wants to live within them, thus developing an intimate and growing relationship, we can lead them to a proper response. In chapter eight, we will flesh out how we are to respond to God's Spirit and his Word by **loving others as we love ourselves and following his ways by making godly choices in life**.

As we've pointed out, studies have shown that this generation is the most relational in history.[1] They love relationships. They thrive on them. Think of the powerful results that are possible when they understand that the God of the universe actually desires to empower them to live in loving relationships with others and make right choices in life every time. It's a marvelous opportunity for us—almost like a bonfire waiting for a match.

FOUNDATION #3: THE GOD OF RESTORATION WHO GAVE US HIS BODY (THE CHURCH)

Sometimes, we can get so caught up in the systems, rules, rituals, and other trappings of religion that we forget the bottom line of what God is really up to. The whole point of all he has done and is still doing is to put things back like he intended them to be in the beginning. He is the God of restoration. He wants to restore the way things were in Eden. He wants to restore that intimate relationship with us that was lost when Adam and Eve fell. He wants to rid the beautiful world he made of its present heartache, sickness, suffering, and even death itself. He wants to bring his lost children close to him so we can experience the unfathomable happiness he created us to enjoy. And he has given us his body, the church, as his instrument of restoration. "God was using Christ to restore his relationship with humanity...and he has given us [his church] this message of restored relationships to tell others" (2 Corinthians 5:19, GWT).

OUR RESPONSE TO
THE GOD OF RESTORATION

We believe that once our young people understand what God is up to in restoring everything to its original splendor they will be motivated to respond by becoming part of the process of reestablishing his kingdom first in the hearts and minds of men and women and eventually in a recreated heaven and earth. In chapter nine, we will expand on how we can lead our kids to engage **in spiritual warfare and reproduce themselves spiritually**. We believe their hearts will thrill at the opportunity to have a part in making the Lord's Prayer become a literal reality: "Let your name be kept holy. Let your kingdom come. Let your will be done on earth as it is done in heaven" (Matthew 6:9–10, GWT).

Building from the True Foundations

Discipling this generation to become true followers of Christ is not a simple task, yet the process can be stated quite simply: **Reintroduce God to this generation for who he really is (the God of redemption, relationships and restoration) and lead it to a continuing response of living a life of (1) faith, (2) worship, (3) prayer, (4) loving others, (5) making godly choices, (6) spiritual warfare, and (7) spiritual reproduction.** Accomplish this objective and you will be raising up a generation of transformed, purpose-driven, mission-focused followers of Christ who know why they believe and how to live out what they believe. The chart at the end of this chapter lays out this objective succinctly, including some powerful results of a generation standing strong in the face of today's culture.

Reaching Their Minds and Hearts

Reversing this generation's distorted views of God, truth, reality, and the church will not be easy. We cannot accomplish it by appealing just to their minds or just to their hearts. We err if we speak merely to their minds, proclaiming propositional truth as if it were separate from a relational experience. And we likewise err if we speak only to their hearts, interpreting the truth as a subjective experience separate from Christ, the person of truth. Our minds and hearts are to work in balanced harmony with each other. We err when we get out of balance either way, and we risk becoming irrelevant to the upcoming generation.

Some have misunderstood my own testimony, thinking that the evidences of the faith alone brought me to Christ. That's not so. It was God's love for me demonstrated through the lives of a handful of Christians that led me to Christ. That love made me realize that if I were the only person alive Christ still would have died for me. Because of what I had seen and experienced in my world, I was a cynical and skeptical young man. Even if there were a God, I didn't believe that he loved me. For that matter, I didn't believe anyone loved me (except my mother, and she had died a couple years earlier). The evidences about Christ brought me to the point where I knew that he was real and all his claims were true: He was the Son of God who gave his life to redeem me. The Holy Spirit used my mind to convince me of his love for me. It was then that I responded to Christ's sacrificial love, and that love became an experiential reality to me as I trusted in Christ as my redeemer.

Some would say that what our young people need is simply the reality of Christ in their lives and that will be sufficient to know that what they experience is true. They suggest that we don't really need to appeal to the minds of this generation. In other words, some would say: "They'll know it's true when it's experientially real to them." But this would play right into the problem instead of solving it. It would cause our young people to base the reality of their experience upon the experience itself, which is at the heart of the error. The experience would have no objective reference point to verify its validity. This is what logicians call a *tautology*—an erroneous, circular reasoning process that uses the conclusion as the basis for the argument. We were not designed to know only by experience without employing the use of our minds nor, on the other hand, is God pleased if we are convinced of the truth intellectually apart from a living, relational experience of the reality that is found in God through Christ. We were created to know with both our minds and our experience.

This is why we must lead our young people to understand the real meaning of truth. Because the truth is true whether one believes it or not.

A Bible college student wrote me after I had spoken on the evidences for Christ being who he claimed to be, and he said:

> Josh, I've been a Christian since I was a young boy. And I was taught that I can know I'm God's child because he's always with me. But I've struggled with doubts because sometimes I just don't feel God in my life. What you shared today has helped me *know he's real even when I don't feel him.*

To experience the feeling that Christ is with you is a wonderful thing, but the problem is that feelings vary. They come and go. Reality, however, does not change no matter how you feel about it at the moment. Therefore, it's important to know the reality of Christ in both our minds and our emotions or feelings. This will mean that in those dry times when you don't feel him emotionally, you can retain your confidence that he is real and he is all he claims to be.

The Holy Spirit uses our minds to affirm the reality of our experience, for as this young man realized, the heart cannot rejoice in what the mind rejects. And when he understood the reality of Christ with his mind, his faith increased. His knowledgeable faith could then carry him through periods where there was no emotional feelings to hold onto. Our young people are vulnerable to any religious wind that blows across the landscape unless we build in them a knowledgeable faith—a faith backed up by the evidence of Christ and his Word.

If you think a knowledgeable faith has little importance in a postmodern age of feeling and experience, consider this. In a recent study called the "National Study of Youth and Religion," thousands of non-religious teenagers who were interviewed said they were raised to be "religious" but had become "non-religious." These teenagers were asked: "Why did you fall away from the faith in which you were raised?" They were given no set of answers to pick from; it was simply an open-ended question. The most common answer (by 32% of the respondents) was *intellectual skepticism.*[2] Thirty-two percent is a very high percentage given the fact that this was an open-ended question. Their answers included: "It didn't make sense to me"; "Some stuff is too far-fetched for me to believe in"; "I think scientifically there is no real proof"; and "There were too many questions that can't be answered."

The culture isn't providing the answers to the religious and ethical questions this generation is asking. The secular thinking is that spiritual matters don't need to be grappled with the mind—you simply believe. In spite of postmodern claims to the contrary, we need to provide clear answers to spiritual questions and our young people will in fact respond to intellectual, evidential teachings about truth. Obviously, our failure to balance the experience of Christ with evidences for the validity of his claims has not helped. Strong teaching on the objective truth of Christ coupled with a "lived-out" faith modeled before this generation is still as valid as it ever was and even much more needed to balance the postmodern emphasis on experience.

Christ, our perfect example, showed that believing is a balanced proposition between experience and knowledge when he said to his disciples:

> Believe me when I say that I am in the Father and that the Father is in me. Otherwise, believe me because of the things I do... the Holy Spirit, whom the Father will send in my name, will teach you everything...I'm telling you this now before it happens. When it does happen, you will believe. (John 14:10–29, GWT)

To believe based on knowledge, as this passage urges disciples to do, does not put reason over revelation; Christ is still the one who determines truth. But it does demonstrate that Christ is pleased when we have a knowledgeable faith. He has given us rational minds. Using our minds to verify the deity of Christ or the reliability of Scripture doesn't diminish the experiential side of having an intimate relationship with Christ and others; it actually increases it.

We call this balanced mind and heart approach to knowing God a *relational apologetic*. Coming into relationship with God through Christ involves a process of steps that follow each other naturally: (1) knowing who God is and why we believe in him, which leads to (2) being discipled in how to respond to him so that we can (3) experientially live out what we believe.

A Shift from Presentation to Process

Far too often, we move our young people from one topic to another in such a fashion that Christianity appears disjointed. Our kids often fail to see the connection between the mix of disparate topics and the ongoing love relationship with God that Christianity is meant to be. The teaching may be there, but at times, it lacks the overarching purpose that motivates a desire to respond. We tend to conduct meetings and courses on dating, sex, drugs, peer pressure, etc. And once we've covered these topics, the sense is "we've been there and done that." It's as if we're attempting to train our kids to live by a set of Christian rules and do the right things one topic at a time. We often fail to tie the rules to the relationship which gives us the motivation to follow them. Rules were never meant to be seen outside the context of a loving relationship. This failure gives our kids the impression that being a Christian is about correct performance and thus contributes to their distorted view of what Christianity is about.

Imagine a marriage in which the only time the husband and wife see each other and express their love is at periodic large-group events. There they sit together, occasionally gaze into each other's eyes, sing songs to each other, and listen attentively while someone describes to them the dutiful performance of husband and wife. At the conclusion of the event, the couple goes their separate ways, only to see each other again at the next group event. That would be crazy, right? It certainly couldn't be called a love relationship, and the rules and songs and meetings would seem to lack real purpose and meaning, giving the couple no reason to take them seriously. But so often that's what our presentational approach to the gospel makes the Christian life look like to our kids.

Being a Christian is not about learning a system of correct performance, but about getting to know Christ intimately for who he really is and responding to him in a love relationship that transforms our whole lives. It involves a process of loving and growing deeper in that relationship so that we as his children take on the characteristics of our Father God and his Son, Jesus. It's about being so intimate with God that we live out those characteristics in relation to one another. Only in that context do the "rules" of Christianity take on meaning and provide sufficient motivation to take them seriously and follow them.

To achieve this goal, many will need to make a radical shift in the way ministry is done. In the eyes of our kids, today's "Structural Church" model often appears to be more concerned about events and making a gospel presentation to a spectator audience than perpetuating a constant relational interaction with God. They simply do not relate to this model. It doesn't translate. We must shift to a "Missional Church" model—one that is engaged in a spiritual formation process with its members, leading them to know the person of God so they can respond to him and become conformed to the image of his Son (see Romans 8:28–29).

The Missional Church

What do we mean by "Missional Church"? The term implies a mission, of course, and our mission is to achieve what we've been describing in this book: to rebuild upon the true foundations of who God is so our young people can experience an authentic relationship with God. We are convinced that once a person really knows God—and we mean *really knows* him for who he is and what he means to us—the kind of response to him that we want our kids to have will be inevitable. If we can reintroduce Christ to our young people regarding who he is, what he has done for us, how much he loves us, and how he yearns to restore all things to his original design, we won't have to cajole them to respond to him. There will be no holding them back.

In the remaining pages of this book, we will flesh out what we have briefly covered in this chapter. We will offer a biblical blueprint for reclaiming not only this generation of young people but also those to follow. To keep ours from being the last Christian generation will require a commitment and concerted effort on the part of all of us. This book represents a commitment and concerted effort on *our* part.

As we stated earlier, we have been asked to help develop a set of resources that will enable you to initiate your own ongoing spiritual formation process with your young people. It is in affect a "Christianity 101" catechism under the banner of "True Foundations—Living Truth for Lifelong Growth." We hope it will not be seen as simply another program. In fact, it is intended to reverse the programmatic approaches and enable you to launch your people into a vibrant and exciting journey to know God intimately and to grow daily in their walk with God. This process will be age-graded (grades 1 through adults) and divided into multiple courses. Full explanations of these "True Foundations" courses and when they will be available are presented in the appendix of this book.

Our goal as a ministry team (and my personal lifelong pursuit) is to partner with you (the church and families) to offer *an equipping and empowering service to help you raise up a generation of transformed, purpose-driven, mission-focused followers of Christ who know not only why they believe but also how to live out what they believe.* Our prayer is that, together, we can do that. And, if we can do that (and we must do it), we can make an incalculable and eternal difference in the lives of this generation and generations to come.

BUILDING FROM THE TRUE FOUNDATIONS

Reintroduce God to this Generation
for Who He Really Is:

The God of Redemption	The God of Relationships	The God of Restoration
Who Gave His Life to Redeem Us	Who Gave His Spirit and the Word to Become Intimate With Us	Who Conquered Death and Gave Us His Church to Reclaim His Kingdom

Lead This Generation to a Continuing Response
to Live a Life of:

1. Faith
2. Worship of God
3. Prayer

4. Loving Others
5. Making Godly Choices

6. Spiritual Warfare
7. Spiritual Reproduction

Empowered to Stand Strong in the Face
of the Culture on the Issues of:

✓ Salvation by grace through faith

✓ Developing a heart of worship

✓ Why truth must be universal and where knowledgable faith fits in

✓ Uncovering the misconceptions of prayer and how to develop a consistent prayer life

✓ How to know God's will for my life

✓ Discovering my self-image and how to develop a healthy one

✓ Discovering my identity in life and how I fit in

✓ Knowing my gifts / talents and how to use them

✓ Understanding and making sense of the Bible

✓ Discovering my purpose in life

✓ How to handle peer pressure and resist ungodly influences (i.e. sexual pressure, alcohol, drugs, addictive behavior, etc.)

✓ How to live a godly life through the empowerment of the Holy Spirit

✓ How to form meaningful relationships with others

✓ What I need to know about dating and how to know I'm in love

✓ How to get along with my parents

✓ How to make right moral choices in life every time

✓ Developing a biblical worldview to see the world as God sees it

✓ Discovering my mission in life

✓ Discovering how belonging and having unity as a group can change my world

✓ Becoming equipped to engage in spiritual battle

✓ How to share my faith and disciple others in Christ

A Blueprint to Rebuild the True Foundation of the Christian Faith

SEVEN
Changing Our Educational Model

"Come, Hanna, Rabban, Elazar," Miriam called. "It is time." She gathered her children into the room, which was lit only by candles.

"We must search everywhere, children," said her husband Ari, who had helped her hide pieces of *hametz* (leavened bread) throughout the house earlier that day. "You must find every piece of *hametz* in the house, and tomorrow we will burn them."

"Father," four-year-old Hanna asked, "what do I do when I find one?"

"Here," her father said, handing a feather and a spoon to Hanna. "Put them in this and bring them back to me, and we will burn them in preparation for *Pesah*, our Passover meal."

"But first," Ari continued. "We must say the blessing." He cleared his throat and prayed. "Praised are You, Lord our God, Ruler of the universe, who has sanctified us through his commandments, commanding us to remove all *hametz*."

"Now!" Miriam announced playfully. "Let's find all the *hametz*." The two boys ran from one room to another in an intense search, but Hanna stayed behind.

"Do I get to ask the big question again this year?" the little girl asked.

"Yes dear, you are the youngest, and you may ask the big question."

By the end of the evening, the game had ended and every morsel of *hametz* in the house had been found. After breakfast the next morning, Ari burned them all.

By sundown that evening, four other families gathered with Ari and his family to celebrate the seder meal together. Once everyone found their places around the table, Ari stood and little Hanna watched with anticipation while a prayer called *kiddish* (sanctification of the day) was recited over the first cup of wine. Everyone then participated in the washing of hands and the dipping of a vegetable into saltwater.

Ari then reached over the table and picked up the middle matzah bread of three and broke it. The small piece he set back down on the plate, but the larger piece he wrapped in a napkin and set aside as the *afikomen*, the matzah eaten at the end of the meal.

"This is the bread of affliction that our ancestors ate in Egypt," Ari said. "I invite all who are hungry to join with us. This year we are slaves, next year we will be free and in the land of Israel." He then sat down and looked over at little Hanna, smiling and nodding to her.

Hanna sat up as straight as she could, cleared her throat importantly, and asked, "Why is this night different?" Everyone smiled in approval. Rabban, Hanna's brother, spoke up. "On all other nights, we eat all kinds of bread and crackers. So why do we eat only matzah tonight?"

Benjamin, one of the other men around the table, answered on cue. "We eat matzah to remind ourselves that even before the dough of our ancestors could become leavened bread, the Holy One revealed himself and redeemed them, as it is written: 'And they baked the dough which they had brought from Egypt into matzah, because it did not rise since they were driven out of Egypt and they could not delay, nor had they prepared provisions for themselves.'"

The evening progressed with the answering of four questions, singing, reciting prayers, and eating. Everyone around the table participated in one way or another. Those who knew what would happen next sometimes smiled in anticipation, and the attention of the younger ones was captured and held by their own involvement and the frequent changes of speakers and activities. Ari finally ended the celebration.

"Let us sing one last song," he said, "with joyful hearts, for we know the ending: The Holy One, Blessed be He, comes and slaughters the angel of death, thereby bringing complete redemption."

Upon the last word sung, each person smiled broadly at one another and shouted together, "Next year in Jerusalem!"[1]

The Hebrew Model of Education

The Passover celebration has been repeated by Jewish families for centuries as a way of passing down to their children the story of the Exodus, the story of the God of redemption. But to Jewish families, the Passover Hagadah ("telling") is more than a Bible story or historical event. It is an expression of who they are, of where they have come from, and a depiction of a specific way of life, a way of being in the world, and a pattern of acting and being Jewish. Through such celebrations, rituals, and retellings, Jewish people absorb not only theology—who God is and how to relate to him, but they also define their identity and underscore the reason for their lives and behavior.

Moses affirmed the process centuries ago when he declared:

> Hear, O Israel! The Lord is our God, the Lord alone. And you must love the Lord your God with all your heart, all your soul, and all your strength. And you must commit yourselves wholeheartedly to these commands I am giving you today. Repeat them again and again to your children. Talk about them when you are at home and when you are away on a journey, when you are lying down and when you are getting up again. Tie them to your hands as a reminder, and wear them on your forehead. Write them on the doorposts of your house and on your gates. (Deuteronomy 6:4–9, NLT)

With those words, Moses was not only proclaiming the truth, he was calling for a "lived-out" truth—a way of life. Moses called for God's people to both orthodoxy (right beliefs) *and* orthopraxy (right actions) in a way that tied the two things intrinsically together, making the truth an integrated, relational part of everyday life.

You see, practically all of modern education, including that of most churches and Christian schools, employs a form of teaching based on a Hellenistic model of education. Greeks shaped much of how we think today about education and disseminating information and truth. Essentially, this Hellenistic approach is to present a student with rational and logical constructs of information that he or she is required to "learn." To determine if the subject matter has in fact been learned, students are asked to regurgitate the information back to the teacher. This is called testing. If the student can accurately repeat the information, he or she passes the course, and the pupil has been "taught."

But the Hebrew model of education is quite different as you can see in the Seder ceremony related at the beginning of this chapter. The goal of the Hebrew model is not mere memorization of repeatable facts; the goal (as Moses made clear) is to *live-out the truth*. In this approach, *truth* is designed to lead to *transformation*. Truth in this educational approach is to be learned by practicing it in real life. According to the Hebrew model, the student has not "learned" a thing when he or she can repeat it to the teacher; it is learned only when it is reflected in the student's life. In this approach, the testing is in the living. The question becomes not whether the student has the information correctly stuffed into his or her head, but rather "how has the truth transformed the student attitudinally and behaviorally?"

The Hellenistic model is adequate, of course, in some areas. For example, certain mathematical or scientific facts are not intended to transform a person's life. However, when it comes to the truth about God and his ways, the Hellenistic model, which many have adopted as their teaching and preaching method in the Church, is woefully inadequate. If we present Christianity as a worldview to be discussed, debated, and proven on a rational basis rather than a transformational basis, we will in all probability continue to see the lives of young people go unchanged. If we hope to reveal God for who he is to this generation and lead them to respond properly to him, we must bring about both orthodoxy and orthopraxy, right teaching *and* right actions in our children and young people. (After all, that is what Moses commanded God's people to do!) Therefore, we must craft a way of imparting the faith to our children that is more like the Hebrew model than the Hellenistic model of education. We must develop a spiritual formation process that not only declares but also demonstrates truth that is continually lived out in relationship to God and others.

As a method of accomplishing this lived-out method of learning, we are suggesting a way of introducing God to our young people that requires an interactive response. Rather than imparting to them cold theological facts about God that they can learn with their heads, we must develop material that can be used to induce a relational response to who God is and what he does for us.

The point of the process is not merely to stuff their heads but to change their lives. And that is what the God of redemption, relationship, and restoration is all about!

EIGHT
Revealing the God of Redemption

"Are you a Christian?" I asked.

"Yeah," Alison responded while standing beside two of her fifteen-year-old classmates.

"How did you become a Christian?" I probed.

"Well, I like went forward in church and prayed and all," she responded smiling broadly.

"Well, how do you really know you're a Christian?" I persisted.

"Hey, I'm no drug head or anything," Alison retorted with a slight irritation in her voice. "I go to youth group; I'm there for my friends and try not to worry my folks too much. I'm not a bad person you know!"

Alison is typical of the majority of our young people. They have made a profession of faith, but few have glimpsed the heart of the God of redemption and experienced a transformed life. Rather than asking students to simply come forward and believe in Jesus, we must help them grasp the heart of Christ as redeemer and then lead them to a proper response. This is critically important today because our young people like Alison have such a distorted view of truth. They think salvation actually results from the subjective believing of the individual. It is a salvation by self-reformation. "If I perform enough good works, I will earn a place in heaven." As previously cited, this view is embraced by sixty-four percent (64%) of our young people.

The truth is we cannot reform or transform ourselves. Even "the law of Moses could not save us" (Romans 8:3, NLT). Why? Because we are dead to God due to our sin. He is holy, and his holiness requires that our sinfulness be dealt with. The tragedy of the human race is that we are all separated from God and doomed forever because of sin (Romans 3:23; 6:23; and Ephesians 2:1). Our young people must first come to grips with this human dilemma.

It is essential that they realize clearly that a miraculous resurrection from death to life is dependent upon Christ being the *one* with the power to do just that. Jesus said that "unless you believe that I am who I say I am, you will die in your sins" (John 8:24, NLT). And there is overwhelming evidence that convinces us that Christ is, in fact, the one true Son of God. That evidence is presented in the courses we have created for youth and adult groups, in chapter four of *Beyond Belief to Convictions* and chapters 5–10 of *New Evidence That Demands a Verdict*. Of course, that evidence does give a rational understanding that Christ's story is true, setting it apart from all other stories found in other religions, but that is not its main purpose. It is there to solidify the conviction that what Christ offers, which is a genuine transforming experience whereby a person becomes a child of God, can, in fact, become a reality. Because Christ is who he claimed to be, what he offers is real and relevant to our lives. Conversely, if Christ wasn't who he claimed to be then his love is not real and neither is his forgiveness. For our young people to be captured by God's redemptive act, they must grasp how God's redemptive heart is both real and relevant to them.

To give you a sampling of how the gospel story might be imparted to young people to reveal the heart of the God of redemption, we offer the following example. It's somewhat lengthy, but I think you'll find it enlightening.

Imagine a youth leader (we'll call him Andy) calling two young people to the front of a room filled with their teenage peers—a boy and a girl, named Chad and Abby:

> "I would like to tell you a story," Andy says, "using Chad and Abby here as a living illustration." Andy then positions two chairs for them to sit in, facing the group. He stands behind them.
>
> "I want you all to imagine this scene," he says. "Chad and Abby here are the first humans on earth. God has just created them and placed them in a pristine, flowering garden, a world that is theirs to keep and tend."
>
> Chad and Abby exchange bashful glances, and a boy in the back of the room speaks up: "If they were just created, how come they're wearing clothes?"
>
> Abby blushes. Andy shakes his head at the group. "They got their clothes at WalMart, just like you did. Didn't you know that on the eighth day, God created WalMart?"

99

The group chuckles politely, and Andy resumes the story.

"The two of you," he says, looking at Abby and Chad, "live in a garden paradise where you can thrive and raise a human family of your own."

Abby blushes again as kids in the group giggle. Andy raises a hand in warning as he continues, "But this garden of yours is more than a physical utopia. It's a land where you live in perfect harmony with one another and with your Creator. You commune with him as a father and as a friend. And that relationship—more than all the fruit-bearing trees, more than all the crystal waters, more than the perfect beauty and comfort of your surroundings—provides everything your human hearts desire. You have love because your love comes from God. You have joy because your joy comes from God. You have peace because your peace comes from God. There is no hunger, greed, fear, or pain because God's holy presence surrounds and fills that perfect place. Then tragedy strikes."

Suddenly, the door to the room opens and a figure dressed in black and wearing a mask skulks in. Andy continues, "A rebellious angel invades your perfect garden in the form of a serpent. He introduces confusion, doubt, and suspicion into your mind, Abby." The figure in black crouches beside Abby's chair and whispers to her. "He deceives you into believing his words instead of God's words. He convinces you to choose your own way rather than trusting God's way. He persuades you to eat the only fruit that God has said is off-limits to you."

The figure backs away from Abby and disappears out the door. "And Abby, that's when you, having sinned against God, add sin to sin. You become a tempter yourself. You persuade Chad to follow you into sin." Abby had been looking at Andy as he spoke, but now she glances at Chad, her eyes rimmed with tears. Something strange is happening in this room. Chad's expression shows that he feels it, too.

Andy continues, "That act—your willful sin against God, in spite of all the generosity and goodness, love, and friendship he has shared with you—results in your expulsion from the garden, the perfect home you've always enjoyed. But it's even worse than that. The consequences are dreadful and devastating, affecting the planet itself—every plant and animal, extending even to every human being who would be born after that day."

"The entrance of sin into your world brought death with it. Your sin severed all your connections to the presence of God. Gone are your shared moments of intimacy and happiness with him. Gone are the thrills of laughter you enjoyed together. Your close relationship, the constant awareness of his love, the sensation of going to sleep in his embrace. All gone.

"Soon you will learn that your sin brought into the world not only the living death of separation from God, but also all the symptoms of death—hunger, disease, hatred, and heartache—symptoms that would only end in your own physical death and eternal separation from God, symptoms that would reign over the whole human race from that moment forward."

All eyes train themselves on Abby, whose face is now in her hands. Andy kneels in front of Abby, touching her gently on the arm. "Abby, are you all right?"

She nods, wiping a tear from her eye. "I'm okay." She looks around the room. "Really. I just got caught up in what that would be like."

Andy stays on his knees in front of her. "As bad as you feel, Abby, God feels much worse about all that went on in that garden. He feels bad for you *and* for all the children born after you in this world because they will suffer the death of separation from God, just as you did. Only, unlike you, they will never have the perfect fellowship you had with him. And the Bible says in Genesis 6:6, that this actually breaks his heart."

Andy stands and faces the group. "God has watched with unspeakable grief as each of you has been born into the very world where he and his first human creations once walked together in perfect relationship."

Andy strides to the front row and pauses in front of a girl. "Anna, he longs to relate to you as intimately as he once did to them." Andy then moves in front of Anna's friend Taylor and looks into her face. "He wants to take pleasure in you." He steps in front of Matt. "He wants to see in your eyes the delight that only his life and love can bring you, but that's not possible because you have been dead to him from the moment you were born, separated from the life that is found in him."

Andy starts weaving through the chairs, sometimes pausing in front of a student, sometimes touching one of them on the arm. "Not only that, but God has been watching from the very first moments of your life as you follow in Chad and Abby's footsteps, becoming his *enemy* by repeatedly and selfishly choosing your own sinful ways instead of God's holy ways. This breaks his heart.

"But his broken heart is far from helpless. Even in the garden, he knew how he would respond. Before the world was created, God devised a masterful redemptive plan (Revelation 13:8, GWT) by which he would enter your world, run to you with open arms and say, 'I love you no matter what you've done, and I want you to be my child again.'

"So God makes his move. *He* takes the initiative. You are the one who desperately needs him, but *you* didn't seek *him* out. *You* are the one who should have been crying, 'Please, God, do something; I can't live without you.' But you don't. You go on in your sin, not seeking or wanting him. Yet he *wants you*" (Acts 17:25, GWT). Andy crouches beside David's chair. "Do you hear that? *He wants you.*

"He wants to reclaim you, to relate to you, to enjoy and delight and take pleasure in a personal relationship with you. So you know what he does? He enters your world to cancel the curse of death that has power over you. The mighty God of the universe 'became human and lived here on earth among us' (John 1:14, NLT). 'Because God's human creation is made of flesh and blood, Jesus also became flesh and blood by being born in human form. For only as a human being could he die, and only by dying could he break the power of the devil, who had the power of death' (Hebrews 2:14, NLT). Do you see? Only the Son of the living God could wrench the power of death out of the hand of his archenemy, Satan, so that God could be reconnected to all creation—*to you*—in a personal, one-on-one relationship."

Andy completes a circuit of the entire room while every eye follows him. "That," he says as he returns to the front of the room, "is the story of redemption. It reveals the heart of God the redeemer. His heart cries out, 'You may have turned away from me, but I'm not turning away from you. You are so important to me that I will go to extraordinary lengths to reclaim you again as my friend and companion. I'll enter your world and become human like you to save you from death and eternal aloneness.'

"God's divine passion to redeem you by entering your world and dying for you," Andy continues, "isn't based on anything you have done or could do in the future. It is purely the result of God's grace (Ephesians 2:8, GWT). Regardless of all you've done or haven't done, he offers you grace. *God accepts you* completely, and in spite of your sin, he provides a way back to him."

Andy stands behind Chad and Abby once more. He places one hand on Chad's shoulder and the other on Abby's. "The gospel story is about Christ, who took the initiative and entered our world when we were helpless, unable to even ask for help, and as your redeemer showed you grace, favor that was not merited at all."[1]

As Andy finishes, he looks around the room. Many eyes are moist, and some faces are streaked with tears. He knows the words have hit home, and he senses this youth group meeting will be different from all those that have gone before.

If It's Not True, It Can't Be Real

As moving as this story may be, none of it means anything if it's not true. If Christ isn't the true Son of the God of the universe, then his compassionate love isn't real and his forgiveness is meaningless. That means his historical birth in a manger and his recorded death on the cross is of no relevance to us at all. However, if Christ did fulfill the prophecies that foretold his coming; if he was virgin born; if he did perform miracles; and if he did raise from the dead, then his story is true, and he is who he said he was. He is God, and he entered the world in human form. If this is true, then it's also true that we are born separated from God, "utterly helpless" (Romans 5:6, NLT). And it's also true that Jesus Christ did become the atoning sacrifice for your sins and mine. "The payment that freed you was the precious blood of Christ, the lamb with no defects or imperfections" (1 Peter 1:19, GWT). The real truth about the God of redemption is that he longed to relate to you and your children so much that he made the ultimate sacrifice...and died and rose again so he could be with you and you with him for all eternity. This is what our children and young people need to understand so clearly.

Our First Response: A Life of Faith

Once we've led our young people to understand the heart of God as our redeemer, we don't stop there. The point of the process is to change the student's life. Therefore, we must induce an interactive response, and this is our next step. We must lead them to reach out in faith and receive his gift of a transformed and eternal life in him. This isn't just a subjective faith that one chooses to believe because the story is emotionally compelling. It is to be a knowledgeable faith that one adopts because the story of Christ as God's son dying for us is absolutely and objectively true.

The overwhelming evidence of Christ's deity and his incarnation is more than adequate to ground our faith in the living reality of Christ our redeemer. He asks us to believe that he has the power to raise us from spiritual death to new life in relationship with him, but he does not ask us to believe that blindly.

God gives us convincing evidences that Christ is his Son to establish clearly that the power to redeem us is not in *our* act of believing but in *him* alone. Our young people, as well as many adults, believe it is faith that saves us. But if faith saved us, then we wouldn't need the God of redemption to do it—faith alone would do the job. The apostle Paul made it clear that "by grace you have been saved through faith; and that not of yourselves, it is the gift of God, not as a result of works, that no one should boast" (Ephesians 2:8–9, NASB).

We have an entire generation that believes that the power of faith is in faith alone. They think the sincerity and intensity of the one believing is what counts. When in fact, the power of our belief rests not in us but in the power of the One in whom we've placed our trust. Jesus placed the value of believing not in the act of belief but in him and him alone. "For unless you believe that I am who I say I am," Jesus said, "you will die in your sins" (John 8:24, NLT). The focus of faith is on Christ our redeemer.

He is the one with the power to transform us from death to life in him, and when we lead our young people to see faith as the arm that reaches out to receive Christ's transforming life, we guide them into a life of dependence on him.

Walking by faith needs to be learned and cultivated into the spiritual discipline of surrender and trust. We will never outgrow our need for a faith relationship with God. Yes, an act of faith reaches out to receive God's saving grace. He has nailed our sins to Christ's cross, and he brings us into relationship with him. But faith in God must continue and grow for a lifetime. For it is faith that engenders trust and surrender as a daily discipline during the uncertainties of life. Faith enables our young people's relationship in Christ to grow and mature even in the midst of heartache, suffering, and tragedy. Once our young people are transformed in Christ, their life in Christ has just begun. Furthermore, if they are to grow spiritually and relationally, we must lead them to engage in an ongoing process of living a life of faith.

Our Second Response: A Life of Worship

They had traveled for three days. The young boy couldn't remember being on such a long journey with his father before. It was exciting.

When his father saw their destination in the distance he told his two servants, "The boy and I will travel a little further. We will worship there and then we will come right back. Abraham placed the wood for the burnt offering on Isaac's shoulders, while he himself carried the knife and the fire" (Genesis 22:5–6, NLT).

Ever since Isaac was a small child, he had seen his family worship God. He had watched animals being sacrificed to symbolize God's redemption and the worship of a singular God. But he was puzzled that this time something was missing, so he asked his father, "'We have the burning coals and the wood, but where is the lamb for the burnt offering?' Abraham answered, 'God will provide a lamb for the burnt offering, son,'" (Genesis 22:7–8, GWT). Of course, we all know the story. Abraham put his son on the altar and prepared to sacrifice him, but God stopped him and provided a ram instead.

Worship of God has always involved the offering of a sacrifice. It began with the blood of bulls and goats and lambs and culminated with the blood of the perfect and spotless Lamb of God—Christ himself. But burnt offerings and the shedding of blood is not what God wants from us. Paul admonished, "Brothers and sisters, in view of all we have just shared about God's compassion, I encourage you to offer your bodies as living sacrifices, dedicated to God and pleasing to him. This kind of worship is appropriate for you" (Romans 12:1, GWT). That's the kind of worship we must lead our young people to engage in daily.

A life of worship to God is about daily sacrificing your interests in all other things and making him your focused adoration. He wants you to love him first and foremost and let nothing come in the way of solely pleasing him. Moses asked:

> What does the Lord your God want you to do? He wants you to fear him, follow all his directions, love him, and worship him with all your heart and with all your soul. The

Lord wants you to obey his commands and laws that I'm giving you today for your own good. (Deuteronomy 10:12–13, GWT)

God knows that if you seek him first in every aspect of your life "then all these things will be provided for you" (Matthew 6:33, GWT). He has the corner on joy and happiness and knows if we live to please him and him alone then we will live a satisfying and rewarding life.

But how do we lead our young people to worship God alone? It begins by instilling into our children—not just as teenagers but even before they can talk—a healthy fear or reverence of God, an acknowledgement of his power and character. As Solomon said, "The fear of the Lord is the beginning of knowledge [wisdom]" (Proverbs 1:7, GWT).

It is no coincidence that the fear of God largely disappeared from our culture at about the same time that relativism and subjective believing became prevalent. Why should you fear a being who you think exists largely because you choose to believe he does? Why respect what you are not convinced even exists anywhere but in your own mind? What this culture lacks, what our youth lack, and what I'm afraid many of us, as parents, grandparents, pastors, youth workers, and Christian educators lack is a healthy, biblical *fear of God*, such as the prophets and apostles knew.

When Moses came near to the burning bush that symbolized God's presence, he was warned, "Take off your sandals, for the place where you are standing is holy ground." Moses obeyed, fell to the ground, and hid his face from God's greatness.

When John the Apostle, who had known Jesus Christ and walked the dusty roads of earth with Him, saw the resurrected and ascended Lord in his heavenly glory, he "fell at his feet as though dead."

Those men loved God with a sacrificial love out of a deep reverence for him, but so many of our young people have a perception of God as a Father Christmas type, dispensing gifts and favor to his children. One young man said God was like his grandfather—a person who didn't really care what he did and left him alone.

How do we lead a generation away from believing there are many gods that could be worshipped to personally sacrificing themselves in a daily worship to the one true God? We begin by restoring the fear of God: "I will put the fear of Me in their hearts so that they will not turn away from Me" (Jeremiah 32:40, NASB).

We are not talking about revealing God as a monster from whom we must cower. Neither do we mean the kind of fear that churns the stomach and keeps people awake, fearful of what God might do. Rather, the "fear" we're talking about is akin to awe. It is a profound awareness of God with a deep reverence and love for who he is and what he can do.

You see, because God has revealed himself as our redeemer who loved us enough to die for us, we need not fear his intentions for us. He has made it clear what angers him and what pleases him. We need to worship him in such reverence as to avoid his discipline and honor his name. Why? Let me give you five reasons.

1. Worship God in Reverence Because He Is God

Like Joshua and his generation who had seen and heard "all the great works of the Lord," we need to reveal the greatness of God to our children. From birth, they need to hear the stories of the mighty power of Yahweh, the God of our fathers who saved Noah and his family from the flood, who destroyed Sodom and Gomorrah for their wickedness, who delivered Joseph out of prison, who sent plagues on the Egyptians, and who parted the Red Sea. Our purpose is to instill within them a reverence for the Almighty, a God of love and mercy. With every story told, every commandment given, every worship song sung, and every prayer offered, we must demonstrate our dependence on God. When we reveal that God is infinite, we acknowledge we are finite. When we reveal that God is all-powerful, we acknowledge we are weak. When we reveal that God is all-knowing, we acknowledge we lack understanding. And in this worship of God, we become profoundly aware that he is the most high God that we depend upon—a God who deserves our reverence.

2. Worship God in Reverence Because He Is the Source of All Good Things

The Bible teaches that "Every good present and every perfect gift comes from above, from the Father..." (James 1:17, GWT). Imagine how it would affect our children's attitudes and behaviors if they really believed that every breath they drew, every morsel they ate, every muscle they moved, every pleasure they experienced, was a gift from a powerful and loving God. Imagine the reverent and worshipful heart that attitude would produce.

3. Worship God in Reverence Because He Is the Judge of Good and Evil

As Solomon wrote, "After having heard it all, this is the conclusion: Fear God and keep his commands, because this applies to everyone. God will certainly judge everything that is done. This includes every secret thing, whether it is good or bad" (Ecclesiastes 12:13–14, GWT). God is a just God and will bring every act into judgment. We and our children need to reverence the God of judgment and worship him as just.

4. Worship God in Reverence Because He Holds the Power of Life and Death

"The Lord protects everyone who loves him," the Bible says, "but he will destroy all wicked people" (Psalm 145:20, GWT). When the children of Israel sang the song of Moses, they proclaimed the power of God over life and death. "It is I who put to death and give life" (Deuteronomy 32:39, NASB). Our young people need to know God as the merciful God who holds their lives in his hands.

5. Worship God in Reverence Because It Is for Our Own Good

God promises blessing for those who fear and honor him: "And they shall be my people, and I will be their God; and I will give them one heart, and one way, *that they may fear me always for their own good, and for the good of their children after them*" (Jeremiah 32:39, KJV, emphasis mine).

When my wife was a child, her father seemed to her to be the most loving and most awe-inspiring man in the world. She loved the smell of his after shave, cuddling in his strong arms, and playing hide-and-seek with him; but she also thought he was the smartest, tallest, and strongest creature on earth. That potent combination of fear and devotion kept her from many dangers. She stayed away from the knife drawer in the kitchen. She played only where she was allowed. She ate her vegetables. You might say that her devotion to her father made her willing to obey him, and her fear made her unwilling to disobey him.[2]

Similarly, God not only wants his children to worship him wholeheartedly, but also to revere him because he knows that such a potent combination will be for our own good and for the good of our children after us.

Cultivating a Longing for God

We must reclaim and revive in our churches and families this worship of the Lord in reverence for the awesome God that he is. We must reverence him, honor him, and sacrifice our own way to follow his way. As Paul tells us, "Those who receive his new life will no longer live to please themselves. Instead, they will live to please Christ..." (2 Corinthians 5:15, NLT). A life of worship to our Creator is about cultivating a longing for God and to please him. We should begin each morning with the heart desire to break a smile on God's face.

I recently read a birthday card from a wife to her husband that could easily have been modified and written to God from the heart of a worshipper:

> Yours is the smile I look forward to each morning, and yours is the voice I love to hear throughout the day. Yours is the touch that can reach my heart and soul, and it's your understanding that calms my doubts and fears. Yours are the plans and dreams that

blend with mine, and yours is the love that means the world to me. My life would be meaningless if you weren't my all and that is why no one has more to celebrate today than I do... Happy Birthday to my redeemer Jesus, my soul mate and my very best friend. I love you.[3]

Imagine your young people feeling this way toward God. Planted deep within our human spirits is a desire to worship God for who he is. He has created within us a longing to connect, a thirst to bond, and a passionate desire to love him. Yet this craving to know him must be cultivated and nurtured into a lifestyle of daily worship. When we lead our young people to truly see God for the redeemer that he is, their hearts will be prompted to know him and love him as the psalmist did: "As a deer longs for flowing streams, so my soul longs for you, O God. My soul thirsts for God, for the living God. When may I come to see God's face?" (Psalm 42:1–2, GWT).

Our Third Response: A Life of Prayer

We want to introduce the heart of the God of redemption to our young people in such a way that motivates them to respond to him in prayer. If they are to develop spiritually, relationally, and emotionally, they must become people of prayer. God speaks to us through his Word and his Holy Spirit. We speak to him in prayer.

In its simplest form, prayer is dialogue with God, yet many people, including our young people, consider prayer a time to ask God for "things." And then they wonder why God doesn't answer all of their prayers. Other questions our kids have about prayer are: "If God is all-knowing and cares about me, why do I even have to ask him for things?" And, "Since God is all-powerful and is going to accomplish his will anyway, what effect are my prayers going to have on him?"

Such questions indicate a failure to understand the purpose of prayer. Prayer is our means to connect with God in order to assimilate his will into our lives. Through an attitude of prayer, God's mind on matters of life can become our mind. "Who can know what the Lord is thinking?" Paul asks. "Who can give him counsel? But we can understand these things, for we have the mind of Christ" (1 Corinthians 2:16, NLT). When we learn and practice the discipline of prayer, it deepens our intimate relationship with God and allows Christ to reflect his character and nature through our lives. Prayer is more than words; it is an attitude of the surrendered heart to be conformed into the image of Christ.

We must lead our young people to learn and practice five types of prayers:

1. The Prayer of Praise

Praising God for who he is puts us in the right spirit and attitude of prayer. "Sing to him. Make music to praise him. Meditate on all the miracles he has performed. Brag about his holy name. Let the hearts of those who seek the Lord rejoice" (Psalm 105:2–3, GWT).

2. The Prayer of Thanksgiving

We are taught to petition God for what we need, but we are to do that within the context of praise and thanksgiving to him. Paul admonished, "Never worry about anything. But in every situation let God know what you need in prayers and requests while giving thanks" (Philippians 4:6, GWT). We need to develop within our children and young people an attitude of praise to God for who he is and a thankful heart for what he has done for us.

3. The Prayer of Confession

Becoming a follower of Christ and continuing to live like him is a process, which means as we grow we often fall short of Christlike attitudes and actions. And that is why we need to offer prayers of confession. The Bible says, "God is faithful and reliable. If we confess our sins, he forgives them and cleanses us from everything we've done wrong" (1 John 1:9, GWT).

4. The Prayer of Petition

"Ask, and you will receive. Search, and you will find. Knock, and the door will be opened for you" (Matthew 7:7. GWT). God is pleased that we ask of him and he wants to give us what we ask. But we must beware of our prayers slipping into selfish requests for things for ourselves that have no spiritual benefit. "When you pray for things," James states, "you don't get them because you want them for the wrong reason—for your own pleasure" (James 4:3, GWT). When our prayers align with God's mind, we learn to ask for what he wants us to have. Thus, prayer helps us to get in sync with God.

5. The Prayer of Intercession

Simply put, intercessory prayer is praying for others. Paul wrote, "Make every kind of request for all of God's people" (Ephesians 6:18, GWT). This type of praying requires a compassionate heart for others. God is pleased that we develop the discipline of interceding for others.

Raising up Sacrificial Followers of Christ

Jesus said, "You must put aside your selfish ambitions, shoulder your cross daily, and follow me. If you try to keep your life for yourself, you will lose it. But if you give up your life for me, you will find true life" (Luke 9:23–24, NLT). Christ wants you and me and our children to give ourselves totally to him. "When you think of what he has done for you," Paul asked, "is this too much to ask?" (Romans 12:16, NLT). Leading our children and young people to respond to the God of redemption is about guiding them to live a sacrificial life of deepened faith, devoted worship, and continual prayer to God. It's about sacrificing a self-centered life and giving one's whole mind, soul, and strength to the redeemer.

The inspired songwriter Isaac Watts caught a glimpse of the meaning of that sacrifice in light of the cross of Christ when he wrote:

> When I survey the wondrous cross
> On which the Prince of Glory died,
> My richest gain I count but loss,
> And pour contempt on all my pride.
>
> Were the whole realm of nature mine,
> That were a present far too small:
> Love so amazing, so divine,
> Demands my soul, my life, my all.[4]

Yet guiding our young people to become living sacrifices to God isn't about challenging them to live an unfulfilling life. Jesus said, "You will find true life." That is because we were created to be fulfilled when we give of ourselves in a relationship with God and others. And that brings us to the next facet of God's heart—a heart that is passionate about his relationship with us.

NINE
Revealing the God of Relationships

Imagine this: You are seated alone in your living room. A large family Bible is open on the coffee table. Suddenly, a radiant light appears. When it subsides, Christ is seated in front of you. Immediately, you drop to your knees and press your face to the floor. His holiness seems to permeate the room and expose your humanity, your sinfulness in such stark relief that you cry out, "Lord, have mercy on me, a sinner!"

In the next moment, you feel a warm hand cup your chin, and he gently lifts your head to meet his tender gaze.

"Beloved," he says, "truly, you were born in sin. You were lost and alienated from me. You had no life, only a lonely, empty existence. Disconnected from my Father—and yours—you didn't know who you were. You felt as if you didn't belong. You were inwardly afraid you would never know who you were or why you were here."

"Then you learned of me, and you trusted in me. And now, because of me, you are God's child. You belong to me, and I belong to you. You are no longer a child of this world; you are the child of the King."

You gain the courage to smile and look deep into his eyes, for you sense he really means it—you belong to him.

He continues, "You are being transformed more and more into the likeness of me because of the gift I have imparted to you, my very Spirit. I have entered into you, and I live there. So I am becoming more and more at home in your heart. And you are beginning to live as you were meant to live—a godly, Christlike life because of my presence within you. You are beginning to experience the abundant, fulfilled life of happiness and meaning, and that brings joy to my heart."

Tears trickle down your face and drop onto the open Bible. "Please, Lord," you say, your voice trembling. "I do want that. I want to be more and more like you. I want to please you. Won't you stay with me and teach me to be like you? I want to see and hear you everyday. I want to have you with me so I can see your example, and maybe then I can be like you."

He smiles and extends a nail-scarred hand, brushing the tears from your cheek. "You don't understand. I have been with you all along." He points to your chest. "I have given you my Spirit, who lives within you. I have given you my Word, too, and I have been waiting for you to see me and hear from me here." He points to the open Bible.

A shadow seems to cross his face, and a single tear rolls down his cheek. "I know you and love you so very much, just for who you are. I know every thought and motive, every desire of your heart. But…"

"Go on. Please go on."

"I want *you* to really know *me*. I never intended for our relationship to be one-sided. I long for you to know me for who I really am—to experience my love, my patience, my joy—all that I am. I want to become more and more at home in your life until you and I are so intimate and you become so much like me that my life is inseparable from yours. That's what I meant when I said this." He points to the page of the open Bible. You pull it closer to you and read. "These things I have spoken to you, that My joy may be in you, and that your joy may be made full" (John 15:11, NASB).

A flash of brilliant light blinds you momentarily. When you refocus your eyes, you are again alone in the room.[1]

The reality is that you and I and our young people are not alone. Jesus is in the room right now, and he longs for us to know him so intimately that we take on his very character and likeness in all we think and do and say. Just as the hearts of human fathers and mothers swell with pride when their child follows in their footsteps or begins living out what they have taught him or her, so our Father God takes pleasure in seeing us become more and more like him.

This relational aspect of the heart of God is one that our young people must know. They miss out on knowing the God who wants an intimate relationship with them because they are not thoroughly convinced in their own hearts that he is the one true God. They are not convinced that the Holy Spirit is real and is available to live intimately in their hearts today. Our task is to show them the heart of God who longs for an intimate relationship with them and lead them to understand the reality of who he is so that they can enter that relationship with confidence. Let's look further at the truths we must lead them to know in order to accomplish this.

God Wants Relational Intimacy

When God laid aside the splendor of heaven and took on human form in the person of Jesus, he revealed his heart for relationship. In that act, he said to you and me "I want a relationship with you, a relationship in which I know you and you know me intimately."

God proclaimed his greatest desire when he said to Hosea, the prophet: "I want you to know me" (Hosea 6:6, GWT). More than anything God wants to restore us to an intimate relationship with him. He wants us to know him so intimately that we become replicas of him.

God created us in his image and his likeness, and even though we have all but lost that likeness because of sin, God has redeemed us so that we may "be conformed to the image of His Son" (Romans 8:29, NASB).

Rick Warren was right when he declared in the opening chapter of his book *The Purpose Driven Life* what the purpose of life is *not*: "It's not about you."[2] Yet the youth culture, even within the church, believes life is about them. We must model and proclaim it's all about *him*, that is, living in intimate relationship with him. It's about glorifying God for who he is by reflecting positively on his character and nature by living like him. This is what gives God great pleasure (Ephesians 1:4–5, GWT).

The very purpose of our existence is to know God intimately...and to become more and more like him.

How God Becomes Relationally Intimate with Us

God wants us to know him intimately, but he doesn't leave us wondering how to do that. He has given us both his Spirit and his Word to accomplish that purpose. Those are the means by which God leads us to become more and more like him. The key is in understanding how God's Word reveals who he is and how his Holy Spirit empowers us to live like him. Lead a generation to become good stewards of the gifts of God's Word and his Spirit, and you will raise up a generation that is a living model of Christlikeness, and you and I won't be the last Christian generation. Nevertheless, it is virtually impossible for a generation to know God and become more and more like him when they are being robbed of the very means of accomplishing that purpose.

"Robbed?" you may ask. "Who is robbing our children and young people?" It is not "who" but "what." The culprit is their distorted view of God's Word and his Holy Spirit because sixty-eight percent (68%) of our young people don't believe the Holy Spirit is a real person.[3] And eighty-one percent (81%) believe it is up to them to create their own truth rather than to discover God and his truth in the pages of Scripture.[4] With such distorted views of God's Spirit and God's Word, our young people are robbed of the means God gave us to know him and live like him.

Clearly, we must impart to our young people a proper view of Scripture. We must correct their misconceptions about the Holy Spirit. We must teach them how to live out the truth in relationship with others. But we must also do much more. We must go beyond presentation to process. We must lead our kids into an experience of understanding *and* living in the power of God's Word and his Spirit. They must understand that becoming a Christian is a way of being in relationship with God and *living* like him through a clear revelation of God's Word and his Holy Spirit—gifts he has given to enable us to know him intimately.

INTIMACY THROUGH GOD'S WORD

Most of our young people do not view Scripture as the authoritative and objective Word of God that reveals who God is and how he wants to relate to us. Instead, they see the Bible as a resource, a set of inspirational stories, and a collection of helpful insights that offers them guidance in creating their own "truth." This distorted view sees Scripture as somewhat of a self-help book to enable them to create their own version of what's true and false, good and evil, and right and wrong.

To reverse this distortion, we need to help our kids understand both the reason for God's Word (to come to know him for who he is) and the reliability of his Word. We must help them see that what we read in the Bible is factually and objectively accurate, and therefore, we can trust it as a revelation of who God is and what he is truly like.

God didn't want us to miss one aspect of what he is like or the written principles and precepts that reflect his character and nature, so he miraculously and meticulously superintended not only the Bible's writing but its preservation as well. Jesus said, "I assure you, until heaven and earth disappear, even the smallest detail of God's law will remain until its purpose is achieved" (Matthew 5:18, NLT).

There is abundant evidence of the overwhelming reliability of the Bible and how it has been handed down from one generation to another with amazing accuracy, and this evidence needs to be shared with our young people. We have created many resources to help you do just that. (See the appendix at the back of this book.)

Coming to believe that God's Word is authoritative and historically accurate is important. But it isn't enough. Scripture is the living Word to be absorbed and planted deep within our minds and hearts. Yet, I know so many ministers and church leaders who study God's Word just to proclaim it to others or to know doctrinal truth merely as a discipline of thought to study and learn. God's Word, though, is to be read and studied and absorbed, first and foremost, in order to know God. God wants us to know his relational heart. He wants us to know that his Word reveals him for who he is, and he wants us to hide those words deep in our lives.

Moses understood this clearly. After God said to him, "I know you by name, and I'm pleased with you," Moses responded. "If you really are pleased with me, show me your ways so that I can know you and so you will continue to be pleased with me" (Exodus 33:12–13, GWT). The Word of God must become a constant companion in the life of a follower of Christ. We must discover for ourselves and instill within our children and young people the discipline of silence and solitude before the Word. Meditation in the Word needs to be cultivated and learned as a regular habit.

INTIMACY THROUGH
GOD'S HOLY SPIRIT

Most of our young people (68%) believe that the Holy Spirit is simply a good influence in the world but not an entity or a person. Scripture makes it clear that the Holy Spirit is a person who literally enters our lives and is there to mold and shape us more and more into the image of Christ. He is there to empower us to think and live like him. Jesus himself said that the Holy Spirit would be an indwelling presence and would lead you "into all truth... he will teach you everything and will remind you of everything I myself have told you" (John 14:17, 26, NLT).

We know that no amount of our own effort or willpower will produce godly living, and yet our kids believe that their own efforts will earn them points with God. We must lead them to discover that the Holy Spirit is there to fill them and to direct them to live daily in the likeness of Christ. We must help them understand that the Holy Spirit is unleashed in our lives through the Christian disciplines of surrender, self-sacrifice, humility, and trust. The Holy Spirit is not something we are to experience only once in our life. He is there to continue to empower us in the process of submitting and yielding to him so that his patience will replace our impatience, his peace will replace our anxiety, his love will replace our self-centeredness, his purity will replace our impurity—and his life will become our life. Paul declared:

> When the Holy Spirit controls our lives, he will produce this kind of fruit in us: love, joy, peace, patience, kindness, goodness, faithfulness, gentleness, and self-control...If we

are living now by the Holy Spirit, let us follow the Holy Spirit's leading in every part of
our lives. (Galatians 5:22-23, 25, NLT)

The key to resisting ungodly influences and living
Christlike is in letting "the Holy Spirit fill and control
you" (Ephesians 5:18, NLT). As your young people see
you personally model this lifestyle of empowerment, they
will come to realize that God the Holy Spirit is a person at
work in the lives of their parents, youth workers, pastors,
and other adults in their church and that they need that
in their own lives as well.

When they come to understand that God desires an
intimate relationship with them so much that he gave his
Spirit and the Word to fill them with his very being, they
will feel compelled to respond to this kind of life and this
kind of giving. What should that response look like?

Our First Response: A Life of Loving Others

When we understand God as the God of relationships,
we are drawn to accept his invitation to intimate relationship by inviting his Holy Spirit into our lives and learning
more about him through his Word. When we learn of his
character through the Bible and yield to his Spirit, we will
be led to respond to God's gift of relationship by living according to his will. What shape does this response take?
The first answer is that we will be motivated to become
more like Christ. We will be led to be the kind of person
to others as he is to us. We will comfort others with the
same comfort he gives us. We will encourage others with
the same encouragement he gives us. We will love others
with the same love that he gives us.

Imagine this scene some 2,000 years ago. A group of Pharisees and Sadducees gather around a radical new teacher and his followers. A lawyer has just posed the question, "Which commandment is the greatest in Moses' Teachings?" (Matthew 22:36, GWT).

Peter elbows Matthew and says, "Hey, this is going to be important. Be sure to get this down because the Master is about to set our ministry priority." Peter pulls the other disciples together. "Now, fellows, listen up," he tells them. "Jesus is about to proclaim the one commandment that will govern our preaching, teaching and ministry from here on out." They all give their utmost attention as Jesus replies, "Love the Lord your God with all your heart, with all your soul and with all your mind. This is the greatest and most important commandment" (Matthew 22:37–38, GWT).

Peter waves the disciples together again. "Alright," he says, "You heard the Master. Our job is to preach a full sell-out to God. We must get people to put their faith in God, worship him with fear, and keep praying to him daily. So let's go, we've got to get this message out."

"Wait Peter," John interrupts, "Jesus isn't finished. He's adding something else." They listen as Jesus continues, "The second [commandment] is like it: Love your neighbor as you love yourself. All of Moses' Teachings and the Prophets depend on these two commandments" (Matthew 22:39–40, GWT).

"Did you write that down Matthew?" Peter asks. "The greatest commandment actually seems to be two! We are to direct our love and worship to God with every part of our being, and then we are to allow his love to flow through our lives to others."

Clearly, the disciples understood that their love for God must be lived out in their love for each other. The apostle John recorded Jesus words, "I'm giving you a new commandment: Love each other in the same way that I have loved you. Everyone will know that you are my disciples because of your love for each other" (John 13:34–35; 1 John 3:11, 14; and 1 John 4:7, 21, GWT).

A follower of Christ is to imitate how God loves us by loving others. It is God's Spirit that empowers us to live out the commands and admonitions of his Holy Word. We are to:

- Love each other (1 John 3:11).
- Be devoted to each other like a loving family (Romans 12:10).
- Show respect for each other (Romans 12:10).
- Live in harmony with each other (Romans 12:16).
- Accept each other (Romans 15:7).
- Serve each other through love (Galatians 5:13).
- Be patient with each other (Ephesians 4:2).
- Be kind to each other, sympathetic, forgiving each other (Ephesians 4:32).
- Place [ourselves] under each other's authority (Ephesians 5:21).
- Encourage each other (1 Thessalonians 5:11).

And that's just the beginning! The Christian life is all about deep, lasting, healthy relationships first with God and then with each other. Think of the many "other" relationships we have over a lifetime:

RELATIONSHIPS WE HAVE
OVER A LIFETIME:

Parents	⟶	Child
Child	⟶	Parents
Grandparents	⟶	Grandchild
Grandchild	⟶	Grandparents
Child	⟶	Siblings
Child	⟶	Child
Child	⟶	Authority Figures
Romantic Boy	⟶	Romantic Girl
Romantic Girl	⟶	Romantic Boy
Husband	⟶	Wife
Wife	⟶	Husband
Adults	⟶	Adults
Adults	⟶	Civil Authorities
Colleagues	⟶	Colleagues
Believers	⟶	Believers
Friend	⟶	Friend
Friend	⟶	Enemy

While we will encounter these and other varied types of relationships throughout life, there is a single perfect model for all of them—Christ and his Word. God provides for us a perfect model for how we are to relate to anyone and everyone on every level that we might encounter. Our task is to understand God's building blocks for relationships and instill them into our children and young people through modeling them ourselves and then guiding them to love accordingly.

The natural question is how? There are numerous materials developed by excellent men and women and various ministries designed to help you instill the process of building godly relationships into the lives of your young people. When we understand the foundational basis that makes relationships work as God designed them, we can teach our children to apply them to their many relationships with others (see appendix).

Our Second Response: A Life of Making Godly Choices

Knowing God's Word and walking in the power of the Holy Spirit enables us to make wise choices in life that are in harmony with God's ways. This is our second response to knowing God as the God of relationships.

God created us in his image and likeness, and we were designed to live according to his ways. Before Adam and Eve sinned, living according to God's ways was a no-brainer. It came naturally and required no thought or decisions. But sin altered all of that, and now we humans must learn to live according to God's pattern of living, which involves our having to make right choices. Making right choices is directly connected to our relationship with God because when we accept his invitation to intimate companionship, he gives us his Holy Spirit to live within us, and it is the Spirit of God that empowers us to make right choices. This both honors God and brings us blessing.

Living according to God's ways simply reflects the way God is, which in turn brings clear and certain benefits. Choosing to disregard his ways, on the other hand, brings clear and certain negative consequences. Moses told the children of Israel, "The Lord wants you to obey his commands and laws that I'm giving you today for your own good...Today I'm giving you the choice of a blessing or a curse. You'll be blessed if you obey...You'll be cursed if you disobey" (Deuteronomy 10;13, 11:26–28, GWT). Our young people need to understand that responding to the God of relationships involves choices that are consistent with his ways so that they can enjoy all the benefits that a relationship with God offers.

This will be a challenge because our young people have adopted the unbiblical belief that "what works is right." We must help them understand the biblical view that because God's ways are *right* they will *work* in life. Making right choices in life actually comes down to whose version of right and wrong we are willing to accept—our own or God's.

During the "Right From Wrong" Campaign, we developed a workbook course that included what we call the "4-Cs Process for Making Right Choices." Many churches and families have used that course to teach their children and young people how to make godly choices. A simplified version of that process is outlined here:

1. **Consider the choice**. God has revealed in Scripture universal standards of right and wrong that reflect his nature. He has decreed that honesty is right and dishonesty is wrong. He has decreed that sex within marriage is honorable, and sex outside of marriage is dishonorable. He has established justice as a virtue, and injustice as a vice.

You and I have many important choices to make in life, but the most important choice is whose version of right and wrong we will accept.

2. **Compare it to God**. The next step is to compare the attitude or action in question to what God has to say about it. It's not a matter of figuring out what's "right for me," it's a matter of determining who God is and what he has said about right and wrong.

   When we decide to compare our attitudes and actions to God and what he says, we are acknowledging that only God is God. When we give up our imagined "rights" to determine right and wrong for ourselves, we admit that God is sovereign and that he alone has that right.

3. **Commit to God's way**. Committing to God's way is easier said than done. First, as we just pointed out, it is uncomfortable to compare our ways to God's ways. It's never comfortable to admit we are wrong. That's why the concept of deciding what is "right for you" is so appealing—it permits us to justify our wrong attitudes and actions.

   Second, even when we do recognize our selfishness and sinfulness, committing to God's way in reality seems almost impossible. In fact, it is impossible to live out God's way in our own power. Therefore, God has promised to empower us with his Spirit to live according to his ways when we submit to him as Savior and Lord of our lives.

135

4. **Count on God's protection and provision.**
When we humbly admit God's sovereignty and
sincerely submit to his Holy Spirit, we can begin
not only to discern the distinctions between right
and wrong, but we can also see God's loving motivation to protect us and provide for us. Living according to God's way and allowing the Holy Spirit
to live through us brings many blessings. While
God's protection and provision should not be our
primary motivation to obey God, it certainly provides a powerful reinforcement for us to choose
the right and reject the wrong.[5]

The Continuing Process

Learning to love others as God loves us and to make
godly choices in life is a process. We don't learn it once and
for all in a study course; we learn it through the course of
life. And the key is to understand that right relationships
and right choices are directly related to our love relationship with God. That is our task: **to reveal the God of relationships to this generation so they might become
more and more like Christ as they become intimate
with him through his Spirit and the Word. The result is healthier and deeper relationships with others and choices in life that are godly choices.**

What else do we need to address? Well, there is something more since not all is perfect. Heartache, pain, and
suffering abound in this world. Leading our young people
to become committed followers of Christ doesn't change
the fact that hearts are broken, tragedy strikes, and people suffer. Or does it? Can Christians actually help change
a world of death and suffering? Could God be wanting
you and your children to engage with him in a mission of

restoration—a restoring of all things to the original way he designed it? That is the exciting mission we want to explore in the next chapter.

TEN

Revealing the God of Restoration

Sixty-five-year-old Thelma sat in the waiting room fidgeting with the magazine in her lap. Her husband of over forty-eight years chatted quietly with a patient next to him, who was also waiting to see the doctor.

"Mrs. Milner?" the nurse called, "The doctor will see you now." Thelma and her husband made their way to an examination.

"Good to see you again, Thelma," the doctor said in a cheery voice as he entered. "You too, Mr. Milner." The doctor made his way to a chair and opened the file folder in his hand.

"Well, there is no easy way to say this Thelma," the doctor said in a serious tone. "The tests confirm you are in the first stages of Alzheimer's Disease."

Thelma's hand instinctively went to her mouth as she let out a slight groan. Her husband grimaced as he placed his arm around his stunned wife.

For the next fifteen years, one of the longest cases ever, Thelma's family watched as her body, mind, and all traces of memory were ravaged by the deadly disease of Alzheimer's. A once beautiful and vibrant woman was reduced to nothing more than skin and bones. Finally, unable to eat, speak, or respond to the voice and touch of loved ones, Thelma gasped her last breath and was gone, leaving behind a grieving family.

Smiles at some point turn to frowns, and laughter gives way to crying. Happiness and health are eventually replaced with pain and suffering. Whether or not a person has committed his or her life to Christ, personal anguish, loss, and death are inevitable. Like the Milner family, all of us will at some point suffer the loss of a loved one. Even the earth feels the excruciating pain of death and dying.

For millennia, the planet has groaned under the stress of a sin-cursed world: tornadoes and hurricanes wreak havoc on life and property, babbling brooks flood their banks to become destructive forces, and the friendly flicker of a campfire is transformed into a raging forest fire, consuming plants, animals, and dwellings. Gentle animals who first roamed the earth in harmony now brutally ravage each other to survive and protect their territory. Mountains erupt, spewing out volcanic ash. Earthquakes topple buildings. The sun parches fields, bringing drought. "We know that all creation has been groaning with the pains of childbirth up to the present time" (Romans 8:22, GWT).

The disruption and decay of this earth and the inevitability of death are a living reality. Pain and loss are felt every minute of everyday somewhere in the world, yet as often as life serves up pain and heartache, we are rarely willing to accept it. Something inside of us says, "This makes no sense," and we hope that life will be better tomorrow. But even if tomorrow is better, it won't mean much because someday all that we have and hold will fade from our grasp, and we will die.

Christ Will Conquer Death

The good news is that the God of redemption and re-lationships is also the God of restoration. God took on human form and died for you and me as a sacrifice for our sins in order to reestablish an intimate relationship with us. However, redemption and relationship are only the first phases of his masterful plan of salvation. Ultimately, God intends to reverse all the effects of sin that cursed the human race and the entire universe in which we live.

The sin of the first couple—and your sin—caused death. "Death spread to everyone, because everyone sinned" (Romans 5:12, GWT). The prince of darkness himself held the power of death over you as well as the entire planet under his control. Only one thing could can-cel this curse of sin: A sinless human not only had to be willing to sacrifice himself but also to have the power to raise from the dead. And that could only be done by God himself. As the Bible records, "Only as a human being could he die, and only by dying could he break the power of the Devil, who had the power of death" (Hebrews 2:14, NLT). And that is what he did. He died for you and me and then rose from the grave to conquer death.

But he is not finished. His sacrificial death and resur-rection has the power to cancel sin, yet "the last enemy to be destroyed is death... Death still reigns in this im-perfect world. But there will come a time when the Son will present himself to God, so that God, who gave his

Son authority over all things, will be utterly supreme over everything everywhere" (1 Corinthians 15:26, 28, NLT). Then and only then will the curse of sin be completely broken and all things restored as in the beginning. A new heaven and a new earth will be created. And, as the Bible declares, the God of restoration will then live with humans. "God will make his home with them...He will wipe every tear from their eyes. There won't be any more death. There won't be any grief, crying, or pain, because the first things have disappeared" (Revelation 21:3–4, GWT). The ultimate goal of God's plan of salvation is to restore his kingdom in a new heaven and a new earth.

You may fully understand and believe with conviction that God's kingdom will one day be restored to a newly created world. You may believe that without Christ's substitutionary death and bodily resurrection "your faith is worthless and sin still has you in its power" (1 Corinthians 15:17, GWT). You may even believe that the restoration of all things is an important doctrinal position of the church. Unfortunately, most of our young people do not.

As we stated earlier, the majority (51%) of our churched youth do not even believe Christ rose from the grave. As alarming as that may be, more serious still is the fact that this distorted belief actually alters our kids' perception of reality and leaves them with a worldview that gives them no true mission in life. Studies show that young people who have distorted views of God and truth are twice as likely to feel pessimistic about life than those who possess a biblical worldview.[1] When we fail to see life—with all its struggles and difficulties—in light of an eternal, biblical perspective, then hope and optimism fade.

Do you realize that 3.5 million kids suffer from depression each year in the U.S. alone, and more than eight percent (8%) of the adolescent population shows signs of major depression in any given year?[2] Two thousand teens commit suicide every year, and another thousand make attempts that are serious enough to require medical attention.[3] Even so, many teens who don't struggle with depression, nonetheless, struggle with feelings of rejection, loneliness, and alienation.

Many websites, blogs, video games, movies, and musicians exploit such teen struggles. Graphic novels depict dark worlds where violence and hatred reign. Musicians like Marilyn Manson and Nine Inch Nails put to music the fear and anxiety many teens feel. Some believe these parts of teen culture create hopelessness, self-destruction, and violence toward others; whether or not that is true, it is inarguable that they capitalize on such things.

Our young people need hope. They need a biblical worldview with a mission in life that will help them weather the storms of adolescence. A biblical worldview is nothing more than seeing life from God's perspective. Our young people need to understand clearly that the God of restoration is calling them to see from his perspective and join him in a mission that literally defines their eternal destiny.

God Gave His Church That We Might Together Make the Kingdom of God an Eternal Reality

God is on a mission to restore all things to their original design and establish the kingdom of God to a newly created earth. He made a covenant with Abraham that the Messiah would come to complete that mission. He promised to transform this earth as well as our bodies to their renewed state. As the apostle Paul says:

> All creation anticipates the day when it will join God's children in glorious freedom from death and decay…We, too, wait anxiously for that day when God will give us our full rights as his children, including the new bodies he has promised us. (Romans 8:21, 23, NLT)

And how is God going to bring all this about? Paul tells us: "We are all one body, we have the same Spirit, and we have all been called to the same glorious future" (Ephesians 4:4, NLT).

The God of restoration has gifted us with Christ's body, the church, to engage with him in his mission to re-establish his eternal kingdom first in the hearts of men and women and eventually in a recreated heaven and earth. The church, God's community of Christ followers, is to bond together as his visible expression to spread both this gospel message and his love. "We are all one body in Christ, we belong to each other, and each of us needs all the others" (Romans 12:5, NLT).

If ever a message will resonate with this generation, it is this one. Our young people long for a community of people who belong to each other and are there to love and support each other. My friend Dr. David Ferguson of Intimate Life Ministries addressed the need for the church to be a relevant and visible expression of Christ's love in his book, *The Never Alone Church*.

Relevance springs from a body of believers who are deeply in love with God and are able to identify a "neighbor's" needs for comfort or acceptance or security or approval and lovingly meet those needs.

Such a message does not ignore a person's fundamental need to be in right relationship with God and love him with heart, soul, and mind. We must love God first; it's the "first and greatest commandment." But we must go further. Jesus always linked love for God with the second-greatest commandment: love for people. An intimate relationship with the God of love, comfort, encouragement, and hope always challenges us to pass along his love, comfort, encouragement and hope to others. That's relevant ministry![4]

Isn't that the kind of body we want to be? Isn't that what we want our children and young people to belong to and carry on into the next generation? The God of restoration gave us his unified body (community of believers) to be there for each other and engage in his mission to reach a lost world. That is the exciting mission we must lead our young people to embrace.

Both the evidence and the first step of God's plan to restore all things is the resurrection of Christ. His resurrection to new life shows his power to resurrect us as well and to restore us to new life. In addition, his victory over death demonstrates his power to overcome the effects of death that are ravaging the planet and to restore it to its Edenic perfection. We must help our young people not only to understand the restorative meaning of Christ's resurrection, but also to realize that it is an objectively true historical fact. There is, of course, ample evidence to establish that fact. (See material in the appendix of this book.) As our young people come to grips with the reality of God's mission of restoration and the fact that the resurrected Christ does have the power to end all suffering and death, they will want to become a part of proclaiming that message. Here's how each of us and our young people need to respond to the God of restoration and to the gift of his body, the church.

OUR FIRST RESPONSE:
A LIFE OF SPIRITUAL WARFARE

John informed us: "The world around us is under the power and control of the evil one" (1 John 5:19, NLT). Taking advantage of Adam and Eve's sin, Satan has moved in and made this world his kingdom, the kingdom of darkness, but God's beautiful creation does not rightfully belong to the evil one. It belongs to God, and it has been willed to you and me and to our children. The restored heaven and earth that God is going to recreate is our inheritance, and God's kingdom will rule there once again. Still, the enemy isn't going to give it up without a fight. "We are wrestling with rulers, authorities, the powers who govern this world of darkness, and spiritual forces that control evil in the heavenly world" (Ephesians 6:12, GWT).

We are in the midst of a mighty conflict, but the primary enemy isn't a godless culture or even wicked people in this world. The main battle is between two kingdoms: the kingdom of this world and the kingdom of God. And we need to teach our young people to adopt a new worldview based on that fact and then equip them to engage in that battle.

A biblical worldview sees this world from God's perspective—as a stolen kingdom temporarily under the rule of an enemy that will one day come to an end. As C. S. Lewis put it, Christians on the earth live in "enemy occupied territory."[5] But their loyalty is to their commander, Christ, who is the leader of a resistance movement to free them from the rule of the usurper. Satan's rule of the earth is temporary while Christ reigns over a kingdom that "doesn't have its origin on earth," as he told Pontius Pilate in John 18:36. While we are under the tyranny of Satan, we suffer, life is short, and death soon claims us all. The apostle James reminded us: "You are a mist that is seen for a moment and then disappears" (James 4:14, GWT).

But the temporary nature of life and the promise of a new kingdom doesn't mean we are to disengage from this present world order. The kingdom of God is to be established first in the hearts and minds of his redeemed children, which means we are to engage in a vigorous spiritual battle to reclaim the hearts and souls of a lost civilization for Christ.

Today's young people may be confused by the thinking of current culture, but one good thing about them is that they are idealistic and willing to commit to a cause they think is worthwhile. That is why they can respond enthusiastically when we present to them the God of restoration. When they grasp the concept of restoration and when they are convinced of the truth of Jesus' resurrection as an initiation of the process, they can respond to the challenge. They will see it as a call to dedicate their lives to something larger than themselves. Our task is to help them understand the situation we are in and the nature of the battle we face.

We have a formidable enemy, and the spiritual battle and our young people must engage in involves nothing less than the restoration of God's eternal kingdom. "You should look forward to that day and hurry it along," Peter says, "The day when God will set the heavens on fire and the elements will melt away in the flames. But we are looking forward to the new heavens and new earth he has promised, a world where everyone is right with God" (2 Peter 3:12–13, NLT).

Peter seems to imply that we can hurry that day along. But how? He goes on to say that "while you are waiting for these things to happen, make every effort to live a pure and blameless life. And be at peace with God" (vs. 14). Allowing Christ to live his life continually through us so that we love others as he loves us seems to bring the kingdom of God closer to reality. Scripture tells us that "the Kingdom of God is not a matter of what we eat or drink, but of living a life of goodness and peace and joy in the Holy Spirit" (Romans 14:17, NLT). Developing a biblical worldview involves seeing this world as God sees it and advancing his kingdom by putting on "all of God's armor so that you will be able to stand firm against all strategies and tricks of the Devil…" (Ephesians 6:11, NLT).

We must help our young people arm themselves for the battle of restoration by learning to live a life of faith, worship, prayer, and love of others and by making godly choices. God has given us his life in order to transform our lives. He has given us his Spirit and his Word to become intimate with him. He has given us his body, the Church, to usher in his eternal kingdom.

When we take full advantage of all these things he has given us, he is victorious through us and the enemy of his kingdom will someday be defeated. "For every child of God defeats this evil world by trusting Christ to give the victory. And the ones who win this battle against the world are the ones who believe that Jesus is the Son of God" (1 John 5:4–5, NLT).

OUR SECOND RESPONSE: A LIFE OF SPIRITUAL REPRODUCTION

Our response to God's mission of restoring his original intent and making his eternal kingdom a reality also includes spiritually reproducing ourselves. In other words, engaging in a mission of drawing people to Christ and leading them to become his followers is helping to restore God's original intent to have a personal relationship with every believer.

Paul puts it this way, "[Christ] has given us this ministry of restoring relationships" (2 Corinthians 5:18, GWT). During the years of Jesus' life on earth, "God was using Christ to restore his relationship with humanity" (2 Corinthians 5:19, GWT). Now, Christ's Holy Spirit is in us ,and he "has given us this message of restored relationships to tell others. Therefore, we are Christ's representatives, and through us God is calling you" (2 Corinthians 5:19–20, GWT). God wants to involve each of us and our young people in his ministry of drawing people to him by the attitudes we have, the things we say, and the way we act. This isn't merely some mission statement we are supposed to believe intellectually; it's a dynamic activity we are supposed to engage in for our entire lives.

Rick Warren in his book, *The Purpose Driven Life*, put it this way:

> William James said, 'The best use of life is to spend it for something that outlasts it.' The truth is, only the kingdom of God is going to last. *Everything* else will eventually vanish.... If you fail to fulfill your God-given mission on earth, you will have wasted the life God gave you. Paul said, *'My life is worth nothing unless I use it for doing the work assigned me by the Lord Jesus—the work of telling others the Good News about God's wonderful kindness and love'* [Acts 20:24].[6]

For many, the concept of evangelism is only to be accomplished in events or one-on-one presentation of the facts of the gospel. Notwithstanding, evangelism should actually be a way of life—an expression of a lifelong mission of restoring people to God and not merely by presentation but by the way we live, how we respond to situations and treat others, and how we uphold truth and values in our own behavior. Evangelism is an ongoing part of a biblical worldview. We can see the truth of this concept in the fact that God is also pleased in restoring others through us when we ourselves are going through times of crisis, suffering, or persecution. It's not that difficult to exhibit love, joy, patience, and so on when everything is going great. But what happens when life seems to go haywire and the storms of life flood over us? When we exhibit Christlike love, joy, and patience in those times, people sit up and take notice. Therefore, those are ideal times for God to reveal his love and joy and peace in our lives. It is at that point when you and I can be a powerful instrument in God's hands to draw people to him.

Patient and joyful acceptance of suffering and difficulty is part of the spiritual formation process we must model and guide our young people to adopt. It will enable our kids to realize that we, as followers of Christ, are destined to live forever with new bodies on a new earth, an existence that is so beyond our wildest dreams that anything "we suffer now is nothing compared to the glory [God] will give us later." For we "wait anxiously for that day when God will give us our full rights as his children, including the new bodies he has promised us" (Romans 8:18, 23, NLT). And that inheritance "can't be destroyed or corrupted and can't fade away" (1 Peter 1:4, GWT).

As we reveal the God of restoration to our young people, we are fulfilling our task of **raising up a generation to join God in his mission of restoring his eternal kingdom by engaging in spiritual warfare and spiritual reproduction**. So equipped, even in the most difficult circumstances, our young people's biblical worldview will allow them to say like Paul:

> We are pressed on every side by troubles, but we are not crushed and broken. We are perplexed, but we don't give up and quit. We are hunted down, but God never abandons us. We get knocked down, but we get up again and keep going... We know that the same God who raised our Lord Jesus will also raise us with Jesus and present us to himself along with you. All of these things are for your benefit... That is why we never give up. Though

our bodies are dying, our spirits are being renewed every day. For our present troubles are quite small and won't last very long. Yet they produce for us an immeasurably great glory that will last forever! So we don't look at the troubles we can see right now; rather, we look forward to what we have not seen. For the troubles we see will soon be over, but the joys to come will last forever. (2 Corinthians 4:8–9, 14–15, 16–18, NLT)

ELEVEN
Be a Process-Driven Ministry

"Oh, isn't she such a beautiful bride?" remarked the lady with the wide-brimmed hat in the fourth row as she watched Melissa glide down the aisle of the church.

"And I can't imagine how much that dress cost," her friend whispered.

Mike, the groom, stood tall as beads of perspiration appeared on his brow. He blinked nervously as he watched his soon-to-be wife come ever closer.

"Dearly beloved," the minister began. "We are gathered here in the presence of God to join this man and woman in holy matrimony."

As the ceremony progressed, the marriage vows were recited, first to the young bride: "Do you, Melissa, promise to love him, comfort him, honor and keep him for better or worse, for richer or poorer, in sickness and health, and forsaking all others, be faithful only to him so long as you both shall live?" After the young groom recited the same vow, the minister finally said: "I now pronounce you man and wife. You may now kiss the bride."

Then came the honeymoon, and following the honeymoon the establishment of a family, the keeping up of a home, and the daily grind of earning a living, of dealing with the everyday matters of life, and of growing in the marriage relationship. But somewhere along the way, we find Mike and Melissa in the marriage counselor's office.

Mike sits nervously tapping his hand on his knee as Melissa speaks.

"I guess we're here because I just feel our marriage has gone stale, you know."

"Why don't you explain what stale feels like to you," the counselor says.

"Well, I don't feel as close to Mike as I used to. When we both get home after work, I feel like he's still somewhere else. When we're together, I still feel there's a distance between us."

"How do you feel about that Mike?" the counselor asked.

"I don't get it," Mike begins. "Yeah, maybe I'm not as touchy-feely as I used to be with Melissa, but I have to work late a lot, and then when I do get home, there are so many things that have to be done around the house. I feel like I do so much for Melissa, I really don't know what else I can do."

"That's the point, Mike," Melissa interrupted. "I'm not asking you to do more for me, just be with me more, that's all."

Mike shrugged, "I just don't know how to give her what she wants."

Relational Intimacy Requires a Process

Many married couples come to the point of feeling emotionally disconnected at some time or another. They experience a wedding ceremony in which they become related to one another as husband and wife. They even become sexually intimate during their honeymoon, but somewhere along the way, many begin to lose the relational intimacy they once shared. And unless they learn that relational intimacy is a process, they will undoubtedly become distant and emotionally disconnected.

Melissa didn't want Mike to *do* more for her; she wanted him to *be with* her more emotionally. Intimate relationships are not sustained by an initial experience or by mere acts of doing for another. Relationships are deepened by learning how to "be with" a person, by giving him or her our very heart, soul, and mind until we become relationally intimate with one another.

This is precisely what God wants of us. Yes, we and our young people may experience his forgiveness and become obedient, but he wants more. He wants us to "be with" him relationally. As Moses said, "You shall love the Lord your God with all your heart and with all your soul and with all your might" (Deuteronomy 6:5, NASB). Yes, he wants us to obey his commandments and live according to his ways. But he wants that for a reason—so that we might be relationally intimate with him. He wants our hearts to be bonded with his heart; he wants our minds to be one with his mind; he wants our lives to be living replicas of his life. Yet that doesn't happen without following through on a spiritual formation process—a process of deepening our relationship with Christ.

What we have attempted to do in this book is identify the steps of that process. In summary, the process is:

- To know the God of redemption who gave his life that we might be reclaimed as his children and then respond to him by learning to live a life of deepened faith, devoted worship, and continual prayer.

- To know the God of relationships who gave his Spirit and the Word that we might have an intimate relationship with him and then respond to him by learning to live a life in the power of his Spirit by loving others as he loves us and making godly choices in life.

- To know the God of restoration who rose from the dead and gave us his church to restore all things to his original design and then respond to him by joining with him in his mission of restoration as we engage in spiritual warfare and reproduce ourselves spiritually.

You may say, "That sounds good, and I think I am leading my people or youth through part of the process, but it's not really working like I want." You may be like me. I need periodic reminders of the process and need to be prompted with specific steps that I can take.

I have found four probing questions that help keep me and my ministry focused on the spiritual formation process and my role in serving others in that process. You, too, may find them helpful as you strive to become a more focused purpose-driven ministry.

Q: Who are you as an individual and what is your ministry?

The apostle Paul tells us, "He has given each one of us a special gift according to the generosity of Christ (Ephesians 4:7, NLT). What are your special gifts? What is your ministry? Do your special gifts fit your ministry? These questions get at the core identity of what makes you and your ministry unique. Until you know who you are individually and have defined your ministry, it will be very difficult to know where you fit in as a leader of others through a spiritual formation process. What deeply motivates you? Are you using your special talents and gifts? What do you do best? Answer those questions, and you'll have a handle on your role in the process.

I have seen so many pastors and youth workers failing at ministry simply because they didn't know who they were—they didn't understand their unique gifting. As a result, they were doing (or trying to do) things that they were not gifted to do. Knowing who you are allows God to capitalize on your strengths, and it enables you to allow others to complement you so your weaknesses become irrelevant.

Knowing what you do best is actually a humbling process because you must come to grips with what you *don't* do best. It requires you to admit that you need others to offset your weaknesses. Some pastors are gifted in one-on-one pastoral care but weak in the pastoral pulpit. Some youth workers are very creative in planning fun activities for the youth yet not gifted in providing solid biblical teaching. Coming to terms with your identity within Christ's body is a process of locking arms with other members of the church to see that each other's strengths are maximized and weaknesses made irrelevant. It is then that relevant ministry can happen because each one is exercising his or her gift and together revealing to this generation who God truly is and leading these young people to a proper response.

Q: Why do you exist as a ministry?

This question gets at the heart of your purpose for engaging in a ministry. Why do you conduct a children's group, youth group, or adult group? What is the very reason you minister? Paul answers that question for us:

> Their [gifted Christian leaders] responsibility is to equip God's people to do his work and build up the church, the body of Christ, until we come to such unity in our faith and knowledge of God's Son that we will be mature and full grown in the Lord, measuring up to the full stature of Christ. (Ephesians 4:12–13, NLT)

Doesn't that sound a lot like leading people through the spiritual formation process that we've been describing? Ministry leaders are there to "equip God's people," "build up the body," and develop "mature and full grown" people in Christ.

It's all too easy for those of us in a public speaking role to think that the task is done once we've delivered our message. The reality is that the task of "equipping" and "building up" the body is usually initiated with a sermon or talk. What happens after the meetings in small group studies and one-on-one support/accountability sessions is so critical. Personally, I don't feel I've accomplished my reason for ministry until small group leaders have equipping resources at their disposal to carry on the message I deliver because the joint task of both my ministry and that of those ministering to others is to foster and maintain an ongoing process of helping people grow in Christ. And unless each of us with our varying gifts work to "hand off" to each other and harmonize our roles together, the process will become disjointed and ineffective.

Local bodies of believers need to understand the means to measure how they are growing in the process of living a life of faith, worship, prayer, love of others, making godly choices, spiritual reproduction, and spiritual warfare. Paul talked about "measuring up to the full stature of Christ." Christ, himself, is our measuring stick. Those of us in a responsible position to lead people through the spiritual formation process need to make him our role model. Our young people and adults will learn from us as we measure up to Christ and in some cases confess how we don't measure up to him. In either situation, we become a living model of the process.

Q: Where are we going as a ministry?

The following question gets at where the rubber meets the road: In what direction is your ministry headed? It is the question that will help you examine whether or not you are on track to fulfill your purpose. Christlikeness is the goal of the spiritual formation process. As Paul stated, the goal is in "becoming more and more in every way like Christ" (Ephesians 4:15, NLT). No matter what a ministry does or how it does it, if it isn't helping to lead people to be more and more like Christ, then its existence and direction need to come into question.

I'm afraid the unspoken direction of many churches and youth groups comes down to numeric growth. Consequently, many pastors and youth workers define their success in terms of numbers. Does a large congregation or a packed-out youth group meeting mean people are becoming more like Christ? Is spiritual growth synonymous with numeric growth? We are by and large a religious and churched culture. Eighty-four percent (84%) of Americans describe themselves as Christian.[1] Amazingly, six out of ten adults (59%) say they worship God everyday![2] But just because people consider themselves to be Christians and are attending church services in record numbers (the highest percentage of adults attending services since 1993) doesn't mean the church is fulfilling its purpose of birthing and developing transformed followers of Christ. According to Barna's research, ninety-six percent (96%) of professed born-again adults and ninety-eight percent (98%) of professed born-again young people do not reflect Christlike attitudes and actions.[3] The primary focus of the true church should not be on numbers but on raising up true followers of Christ.

This isn't to say a ministry shouldn't experience numeric or even financial growth, but the focused direction of a process-driven ministry is not toward attendance or dollars. It's about revealing God for who he is and leading people to a proper response to him so they can become more like Christ. To keep your ministry on track, keep asking yourself, "Where are we going?" When you purchase Sunday school material, church class studies, or small group curriculum ask yourself, "Will this take us where we want to go?" If it doesn't, find material that will help you get there.

Q: How are we going to get there as a ministry?

When you understand your unique identity, your purpose, and your direction, you are ready to draft a process-driven plan. But you can't get there alone. You need others of like heart and mind. That is at the core of the body concept; we don't do ministry alone. You must lock arms—and hearts—with others and plan how you're going to equip and lead people through a spiritual formation process. As Paul said, "As each part does its own special work, it helps the other parts grow, so that the whole body is healthy and growing and full of love" (Ephesians 4:16, NLT).

Ministries that develop effective plans to equip people to live Christlike lives are:

1. Ministries where people understand who they are and what they do best;
2. Ministries where people have a clear understanding of how to share who Christ is, what he offers, and specifics of how a person should respond to him in every aspect of life;
3. Ministries that have developed living models of what Christ looks and sounds like and then challenge, equip, and empower people to become more and more like Christ.

A process-driven ministry is about equipping people to live and grow and become more and more in love with God and others. It's really about the process, the journey we are all on to become more intimately connected with Christ, and there are certain characteristics of those kinds of ministries, which is the topic of the next chapter.

TWELVE
Characteristics of a Process-Driven Ministry

We have stressed how important it is that each of us in ministry know who we are, why we're here, where we're going, and how we're going to get there. The next step is to identify the core characteristics of a process-driven ministry and to build them into a plan. Although such a ministry may have many characteristics, we have identified five that are critically important and stand out above all others. More than things we must do, these characteristics show what we must become if we are to truly lead a process-driven ministry that results in people "becoming more and more in every way like Christ."

1. Process-Driven Ministry is Mission-Focused

Being mission-focused keeps our eyes and hearts on the process of reaching the lost and equipping the saints. Leading people through the spiritual formation process becomes our mindset. We measure everything we do through that grid. This is in contrast with a "structural church" mentality that focuses primarily on events and programs. Being a "missional church" is being a body of believers who answer the critical questions we covered in the previous chapter. A missional church has a clear purpose for meeting together as a body of Christ. In some cases, that purpose will be to worship (celebrating Christ for who he is and what he has done for us). Other meetings may indeed focus on teaching and training, although not teaching and training for its own sake. Such a church knows what characteristics of God and Christ it is going to reveal to its people and knows the specific responses it wants to lead its people through.

Small groups, or growth groups as they are sometimes called, provide some of the best forums for mission-focused ministry. They provide time for people to learn from each other and share how they are learning to live out their spiritual formation discoveries in everyday life. Group assignments and exercises can be handed out during each small group session and then discussed the next week. Such gatherings are the heart of the missional church. There are close to a million small groups meeting in the United States every week over and above Sunday School classes. Fifty-three percent (53%) of evangelicals attend a Sunday School each week, yet sixty-one (61%) percent attend a small group meeting during the week.[1] Take advantage of that phenomenon to establish a spiritual formation process within those small groups.

One pastor was successful in getting many of his people involved in home groups, but he was disturbed to find that much of the meeting time was spent with people sharing their subjective ideas of what various scripture passages meant to them. Therefore, he came up with a plan.

He launched a sermon series exploring a specific book of the Bible. Each week, he printed out discussion questions based on the passage he explored in his Sunday morning sermon and distributed them to the church's small groups. His weekly sermon set the stage and provided crucial context and solid exposition of the passage for the small group studies. Over time, his initiative gave birth to new groups until his church had over eighty small groups per week, all studying the scripture passage the pastor spoke on each Sunday morning. People were challenged to live out the Christlike characteristics they were discovering in their groups, and the church doubled in size (to over three thousand) in just one year.

Not everyone, of course, can implement that method and achieve the same results. Every situation is different, and each requires approaches that fit its unique needs. But everyone who maintains a mission-focus in the spiritual formation process can expect results. The key is to grasp the spiritual goals clearly and carefully define the process you want your people to pursue in order to achieve the goal.

Being mission-focused means challenging every program, curriculum, or event you wish to launch by asking the tough questions:

- "What is this program or event going to accomplish?"
- "Is it going to help me lead people through a process?"
- "How is it going to help my people become more like Christ?"

You don't have to be a genius to ask those questions, but before you can answer them, you do have to know the spiritual formation process through which you want to lead your congregation or group. Thus, when various ministries, publishers, or groups want you to use their products, resources, or events you can ask:

- "How does it help me equip my children, youth, or families to deepen their faith or worship of God or be more effective in their prayer life?"

- "How does it train them to unlock the truths of God's Word and walk in the power of the Holy Spirit to express their love for others or make godly choices in life?"

- "How does it teach them to spiritually multiply themselves or develop a biblical worldview to make God's eternal kingdom a reality?"

A ministry that is mission-focused will use only materials and processes that focus on the task of developing authentic followers of Christ who live Christlike lives.

2. Process-Driven Ministry Models Christlikeness

Our children and young people need models, people who demonstrate what a follower of Christ sounds and looks like. A process-driven ministry must be composed of people who are such models. Paul obviously endorsed this concept when he said, "Brothers and sisters, imitate me, and pay attention to those who live by the example we have given you" (Philippians 3:17, GWT). He amplified that idea when he told Timothy, "Don't let anyone look down on you for being young. Instead, make your speech, behavior, love, faith, and purity an example for other believers" (1 Timothy 4:12, GWT).

Being models to our children and young people doesn't mean being perfect. No one is absolutely perfect, of course, but our kids do need to see in us living examples of what true followers of Christ are like.

Recently, I was interacting with two gentlemen who disagreed with me as to how we should do something. The conversation became heated, and one of these men spoke rather harshly to me. Later in the day, he came to me and the other person and apologized, saying, "During our time together, I felt threatened and feared that the plans I was putting in place would be derailed. I became defensive and disrespectful of you both. That was wrong of me. It was very unChristlike. I hurt you and I am sorry. Please forgive me."

Now, this man's earlier actions were far from being a perfect model of Christlikeness, but he was, nonetheless, a model of one who was truly following Christ because he was sensitive to the convicting Spirit of God when he offended another brother.

Believe it or not, our kids actually need to see us fail and seek forgiveness. They need to see us humble ourselves and realize that we, too, are in the process of "becoming more and more in every way like Christ." None of us has arrived (and we won't "arrive" until we're glorified). But our children and young people still need to see the spiritual formation process as a lifelong journey of becoming more and more like Christ, and they need us to model that journey before them. We never outgrow our continual need to deepen in our faith, worship, prayer, dependence upon God's Word, submission to his Holy

Spirit, love of others, and so on. If the church is to survive into the next generation, we must model before them living examples of authentic followers of Christ.

One of the big pluses of process-driven ministry is that it provides a format for this kind of modeling to occur. That is the importance of intergenerational ministry.

3. Process-Driven Ministry is Intergenerational

We live in an age of the two-wage-earner household in which young people spend mere minutes a day in meaningful conversation with their parents. Gone is the day when extended family members sat around the fireplace interacting with each other. Fifty-five years ago, some sixty to seventy percent (60-70%) of all households included at least one live-in grandparent; today less than two percent (2%) of households benefit from that resource.[2]

Intergenerational activity has virtually become a thing of the past, and we as a culture are experiencing the consequences. We have lost the benefit of wisdom coupled with love that comes from regular contact with grandparents. As a result, we miss the sense of heritage, connectedness, and continuity with the past that intergenerational contact provides. Unfortunately, contact is lacking not only between kids and grandparents but also between kids and their parents. The hectic schedules and expectations of our culture conspire to minimize contact even between adjacent generations. This causes most of our youth today to feel disconnected and alienated from an adult world, and unless we correct this, we as adults will be unsuccessful in our attempts to instill our faith and values into the next generation. Values don't tend to root solidly when they are merely taught; they must be *caught*, like a good infection, from constant contact with loved and respected people who are carriers.

Intergenerational ministry is nothing more than a ministry that brings adults, children, and youth together and teaches them how to interact and learn the spiritual formation process from each other. It will not be enough to provide instruction to parents and expect them to go home and parent effectively. Many young parents today are without parenting models. Churches can take a giant step toward saving future generations of Christians by bringing parents and children and teenagers together at church-sponsored meetings and providing on-the-job parental training.

Imagine, for example, parents attending children's church on occasion. They would experience the process of entering into their child's world and interacting with them in meaningful ways. A parent might learn how to be vulnerable about feeling sad and lonely as he shares with his child his memory of losing a friend. Imagine a father saying to his six-year-old son: "I remember when I was six my best friend moved away. I was really sad, and I cried. As I think of it now, it still saddens me." Imagine this father's child being told that he can comfort his dad by feeling sad with him and expressing that with a warm hug. Both father and son experience the meaning of Romans 12:15, "Be sad with those who are sad," as a bonding between them takes place.

This is but one example of the type of on-the-job training parents can experience when they turn from programs to process. Parents can learn through actual experience how to show attention to their children, express acceptance without judgment, comfort a sad child, and meet a child's need for affection, appreciation, encouragement, security, and respect. Parents of teenagers can learn skills such as how to be positive and how to reassure and support young people as they enter into the awkward years of adolescence.

Imagine parents and teens being instructed in separate groups on the skill of self-disclosure so they can communicate how they truly feel. Then as they come together, think how a mother could share directly with her daughter how she failed to make the cheerleading team when she was in high school as the entire group observes and learns. The young girl begins to realize, *Hey, maybe my mom does understand some of what I'm going through.* Consider the life-changing experience of a teen as a dad shares how he feels inadequate as a father and confesses a particular time when he became impatient and got angry with his teenager. Imagine the impact on a teen as he or she hears a parent share how he or she wants to learn better how to yield to God's Holy Spirit in those situations so that Christ's patience and tenderness will become their own characteristics. As children and young people begin to see spiritual formation take place in their parents, they will begin to be led through the process themselves.

Intergenerational ministry will be no easy task, especially at first, because of the way most local churches and ministries are structured. Many churches will need to adjust their thinking if they are to become truly missional churches.

Some time ago, we met with approximately fifty denominational and parachurch leaders to address this very issue. The combined years of ministry experience of that group exceed three hundred years. With that much experience in the room, we hoped some insight would be forthcoming on intergenerational ministry. And it was.

We proposed three questions to these experienced, insightful men and women:

- What are the benefits of intergenerational ministry?
- What are the obstacles to intergenerational ministry?
- How do we overcome the obstacles of intergenerational ministry?

Here's how this prestigious group corporately answered these questions:

WHAT ARE THE TOP 10 BENEFITS OF INTERGENERATIONAL MINISTRY?

(IN ORDER OF PRIORITY)

1. A mutual imparting of wisdom, creating a higher understanding and engendering trust.
2. Increased communication between adults and youth.
3. Opportunity for mentoring, guidance and modeling.
4. Reduced fear.
5. Increased intimacy and connectedness.
6. Increased oneness and unity.
7. Greater feeling among youth of being valued and heard.
8. Creation of a safe place where love grows.
9. Stronger family units.
10. Greater vitality as older adults derive energy and enthusiasm from youth.

These are impressive advantages, enough to make us wonder why more churches and ministry groups haven't been pursuing intergenerational ministry more aggressively. That's why we asked the same group about the major obstacles they saw to intergenerational ministry.

WHAT ARE THE TOP 10 OBSTACLES TO INTERGENERATIONAL MINISTRY?
(IN ORDER OF PRIORITY)

1. Resistance or fear of change.
2. Fear of disclosure, intimacy, having to face reality.
3. Busyness and over-commitment (i.e., intergenerational ministry "requires too much work").
4. A lack of training and leadership personnel.
5. Church structure and traditions.
6. Fear of inadequacy, especially among fathers.
7. Unresolved conflicts in family, lack of trust, and respect.
8. A lack of prioritization by both church and family.
9. Suspicion (i.e., fear that intergenerational ministry is too "different" or maybe even heretical).
10. Failure to see the cultural relevance.

With such an array of obstacles, it's easy to understand why so few churches and ministries seem eager to pursue intergenerational ministry. But the same group with three thousand years of combined experience, nonetheless, saw numerous ways to overcome the greatest obstacles.

HOW DO WE OVERCOME THE TOP 5 OBSTACLES OF INTERGENERATIONAL MINISTRY?

1. Overcoming resistance or fear of change.
   - Expose the need possibly through workshops and sermon material.
   - Educate on the benefits, give testimonials.
   - Start with church leadership.
   - Begin with pilot program on small scale and build from there.
   - Provide training.
2. Overcoming fear of disclosure, intimacy, or having to face reality.
   - Develop a biblical teaching that addresses each fear.
   - Let leadership take the lead in being transparent and vulnerable.
   - Provide a teaching series for the pulpit, the classroom, and the home.
   - Focus on personal intimacy with God first.
   - Emphasize similarities and common ground among adults and youth rather than differences.
   - Generate a mission statement on intergenerational ministry among youth and adults.
   - Bathe the ministry in prayer.
3. Overcoming the obstacle of being too busy.
   - Identify the priorities of the church.
   - Define what is essential.
   - Let leadership model priorities.

- Integrate or replace existing ministry/programs with intergenerational ministry/programs.

4. Overcoming a lack of training.
    - Convince pastors of the need.
    - Identify lay couples within church willing to accept the challenge of intergenerational ministry.
    - Send interested lay couples to training seminar on intergenerational ministry.
    - Make resources available.

5. Overcoming the church structure that is not set up for intergenerational ministry.
    - Must begin in the heart of the pastoral leadership.
    - Raise consciousness of need with the local congregation—cast a vision.
    - Include intergenerational ministry in the "purpose statement" of church.
    - Begin slowly with a process.
    - Adopt in a small group first to establish a working model.
    - Commit intergenerational ministry in prayer.

These are obviously excellent steps to take, though, of course, you may not be able to implement all of them at once. (In fact, it wouldn't be wise to do that.) But we must begin somewhere; we can no longer afford to maintain our blind allegiance to a Hellenistic model of education. We must move our churches and ministries beyond mere proclamation into process, beyond mere programs to a clear purpose. We must transition into a holistic, Hebrew way of leading our kids into the reality and relevance of the truth and restore to them a living model of what a committed follower of Christ looks like. It may not be accomplished all at once, but it must be done, and judiciously introducing these changes will eventually produce results.

Resources are available to help with the transition. Dr. David Ferguson's Intimate Life Ministries of Austin, Texas, has developed excellent training for intergenerational ministry. They are able to point to scores of successful models of such ministry in church after church. In addition, our own ministry team has developed the workbook courses for adults as a practical first step in intergenerational ministry (see appendix). These are great places to start.

4. Process-Driven Ministry is Risk-Taking and Revolutionary

It was a revolution waiting to happen. In the latter years of the eighteenth century, the American colonies became increasingly frustrated with policies and taxes imposed by England that made colonial life and commerce increasingly difficult. The estrangement between the crown and the colonies widened month-by-month until the first shots of the American Revolution were fired at Lexington, Massachusetts, in 1775. The revolution raged for six-and-a-half years, ending with the surrender of General Lord Cornwallis at Yorktown, Virginia, on October 19, 1781.

That revolution—like most revolutions—exploded out of a deep and widespread dissatisfaction with the status quo: high taxes, poverty, oppression, and inequality.

People were not just a little gloomy; they were incensed, infuriated, and angry enough to risk discomfort, danger, and even death to bring about a change.

We need risk-taking revolutionaries who believe enough is enough and are ready to do something about it. A friend and colleague, David Hone, has said that significant change only takes place when there is: (1) adequate external pressure; (2) sufficient internal dissatisfaction; and (3) a positive model or blueprint for change.

No doubt you have felt the external pressure of a godless culture and its negative influence on your kids and family. No doubt you have felt the internal dissatisfaction from friends and family (and within the church) that something must be done or the church may not survive our own generation. And we trust we have offered you a starting point, at least, for a positive and practical blueprint for change.

No doubt about it, process-driven ministry is revolutionary. It defies the status quo. It involves risk to implement and maintain it. We urge you to show courage. Step out and speak up as an agent for a spiritual revolution.

One thing you can do to get started is to obtain five copies of this book, give them to five key families in your church, including your pastor and youth worker, and request a meeting. If you go to *www.TrueFoundations.com/ meeting*, we will provide you with a step-by-step instruction form outlining how to conduct your first meeting. Committing to meeting with the key leaders of your fellowship can become your first step toward inciting a God-sent spiritual revolution in the way you do ministry.

5. Process-Driven Ministry Builds Community Coalitions

We do not always find strength in mere numbers, but we do always find strength in a number of people who are united together in a common purpose. Wise Solomon said, "Two people are better than one because together they have a good reward for their hard work. If one falls, the other can help his friend get up" (Ecclesiastes 4:9–10, GWT).

Churches around this country and around the world need to unite together in communities without losing or compromising their distinctives. Many of the reasons there are so many evangelical denominations and church groups are legitimate (style of worship, theological differences, governmental preferences, etc.), but we have far deeper things in common that unite us, making those few things that divide us insignificant by comparison. We have far more in common than we usually acknowledge, and there is far more room (and reason) for cooperation than we can often imagine. Bringing church leaders together in your area to address the crisis will bring urgency to the issue…and wisdom to the table.

But you may be thinking, "How do I do that?" Again, we will provide you with the needed aid to help you accomplish it. If you go to *www.TrueFoundations.com/coalition*, we will provide you with specific instructions on how to initiate a coalition in your area. On that website is a form that will guide you step-by-step through the process of building a coalition in your area.

THIRTEEN
We Want to Serve You

We began this book by stating that our goal is to help you in reaching your goals. If you identify with the need to become more of a process-driven ministry, there are five areas in which we would be honored to serve you. A couple of these areas are in the initial stages of development, so it will take time for them to be fully functional, and we welcome your advice and interaction in helping us develop these areas into better equipping and empowering services to help you on the local level. Let's explore these five areas one-by-one:

- **An Ongoing Interactive Connection**

Through the innovative technology of the internet, you and I can be connected in ways we could only have dreamed of in years past. We can learn of your struggles and successes and pass those on to others for encouragement and guidance. We can provide you instant downloadable research, sermons, devotionals, and group lessons. You can start your own e-prayer group that allows your prayer partners to post and receive prayer requests, devotionals, and other messaging. All of this is now possible at *www.TrueFoundations.com/e-connection,* formerly *BeyondBelief.com.* We plan to develop interactions and applications as such resources grow and we adapt to the needs of our growing online community. Our hope is that we connect with you and stay connected so that we will be able to serve you better.

• Hebrew Model Training

If there is one thing we hear from those in ministry, especially from youth leaders, it is their sense of feeling inadequate for the great task to which they're called. That may be your sentiment, too. But what if there were a person in your area to whom you could go for instruction, training, and mentoring in the Hebrew model of education? That is precisely what we want to provide. Our goal is to have certified True Foundation Trainers in every major area of the country to be your personalized mentors in youth ministry, eventually expanding into children's and adult ministry.

Additionally, what if you could actually go someplace for a few days or a week and literally see effective ministry modeled. What if you could sit under the brightest and most innovative specialists on youth issues? This, too, is something we hope to provide in the months to come as our "True Foundations" efforts take flight. We envision a "True Foundations Institute" where mentors can help you clearly answer the ministry questions of, "Who are we? Why are we here? Where are we going?" and "How are we going to get there?" Our plans also include the opportunity for you to become qualified as a certified "True Foundations" trainer to your community of youth workers.

For the time being, however, we are referring you to others who have various types of specialized training. Go to *www.TrueFoundations.com* and click on "training." There you will be updated as to our progress on providing training and find a list of numerous ministries that offer training.

- ## Coalition Based Community Events

As we have stated, one of our big challenges is in changing the prevailing models and systems within ministry. Most churches are presently event-driven rather than process-driven. Since we have made a case for change, you might ask why would we be offering the services of events? Because events are still vital *if* and *when* the events are clearly seen as means to an end and not as ends in themselves.

What is the general state of mind when people emerge from events conducted under an event-driven ministry mentality? In most cases, people sense they have done their duty by attending the meeting and hopefully received beneficial instruction and inspiration for the day. Event-driven ministry can't expect much different from their people because the event is so often perceived as an end in itself. Process-driven ministry, however, sees events differently. The event is a means to an end, and that end is revealing God for who he is and leading people to properly respond to him by living the truth out in relationship with others.

It's not that events are not important because they are vitally important. Scripture states, "We should not stop gathering together with other believers" (Hebrews 10:25, GWT). The point is that those events must serve the over-all purpose of guiding people through the spiritual formation process. And coalition-based community events can help tremendously in the realignment from event-driven ministry to process-driven ministry.

In order to initiate events that are process-driven, we encourage you to take the initiative and either join an existing coalition or form one if your area doesn't have one. Ministries like First Priority or the National Network of Youth Ministries are groups that are pulling together a broad-based evangelical coalition in community after community. These ministries can help you form a coalition of churches in order to serve the Christian community with process-driven events. One huge benefit of such community coalitions is that they bind concerned churches together in a common cause, giving them the opportunity to form a consensus on the vital task of revealing who Christ truly is to this generation and leading these young people to a proper response.

After forming a coalition, your next step is to develop an action plan outlining what you as a coalition can do to initiate and perpetuate the process. For example, make plans to host process-driven events jointly with other churches in your community that see events as a launching pad for spiritual renewal rather than simply an end in themselves. Our own tour team requires that a coalition of broad-based ethnic and theologically diverse groups be formed before we schedule the tour in a community.

We do this because the events are not for us; they are for each church to gain ownership in order to perpetuate the spiritual formation process within its group.

Your coalition of churches and parachurch ministries should dictate the kind of events that come to your area. Once your coalition is respected for its strength and diversity, it can be seen as a valuable service to all the evangelical churches in your area because you are providing training, modeling, and mentoring to move the churches in your area from program to process. Again, we remind you that you can learn how to form a local coalition and schedule a series of events in your area by going to *www.TrueFoundations.com/coalition.*

- **Process-Driven Resources**

Events can be highly motivational, inspirational, and a time of challenge and decision for every participant, yet if the motivation, inspiration, challenge, and decisions from the event are not acted upon, the value of the event is greatly diminished. That is where process-driven resources can help enormously. When you purchase resources (discipling products) that are process-driven, especially small group courses, you are investing in the lives of your people because process-driven resources are designed to challenge and equip them to live out the truth in their everyday lives. And when you follow up a highly challenging event with a complementing process-driven course, you maximize the event and lead your people to practice daily what they've seen and heard.

We have developed a family of process-driven resources under the banner of "True Foundations—Living Truth for Lifelong Growth." These resources are for all age groups to be used by children's workers, youth workers, pastor/adult group leaders, and parents. They are designed both to help you rebuild the foundations of the faith and to initiate the spiritual formation process we've been discussing in this book. These resources are listed in the appendix of this book, or again, you can go online to *www.TrueFoundations.com/resources* and review them.

Of course, this family of resources will not provide every single thing you will ever need to raise up a generation to be spiritually, emotionally, and relationally healthy and mature, but it provides what we believe to be the foundational starting point that forms the basis for becoming more and more like Christ.

Our plan is to partner with other people and ministries as your needs arise to address more specialized areas for children, youth, and adults. We want to learn more and more of what you need and then provide "True Foundations" resources to meet those needs.

• Global Mobilization

We in North America have so much for which to be grateful. In fact, to be honest, most of us are more spoiled than we realize. But there are dedicated followers of Christ around the world who need the "True Foundations" events, resources, and training perhaps more so than many here in this country. Our goal is to reach them with this message, too.

Presently, for every one of our books that are sold in North America, two are distributed in a foreign country. Most of the resources we have produced over the last thirty-three years have been translated into other languages—twenty-four million books in over seventy-five languages. Our heart's desire and fervent goal is to continue to serve those faithful followers of Christ in other countries, many of whom suffer persecution for their faith. We have produced translations of our books in numerous languages, but we want more than that; we want to work with various Christian groups in foreign countries so that they, too, can offer events and training. If you know of someone in a foreign country whom you think would be interested in launching this effort to rebuild the foundations of the faith within their country, simply give us their e-mail address at *www.TrueFoundations.com/global*, and we will make contact with them.

A CLOSING PRAYER

There is no more fitting conclusion to this book than the prayer Paul penned some two thousand years ago. This is our sincere and heartfelt desire for you as you faithfully minister and become more of a process-driven ministry to raise up this generation to become transformed followers of Christ so that we will not be the last generation of true Christians in this country:

> I pray that from his glorious, unlimited resources he will give you mighty inner strength through his Holy Spirit. I pray that Christ will be more and more at home in your hearts as you trust in him. May your roots go down deep into the soil of God's marvelous love. And may you have the power to understand, as all God's people should, how wide, how long, how high, and how deep his love really is. May you experience the love of Christ, though it is so great you will never fully understand it. Then you will be filled with the fullness of life and power that comes from God. Now glory be to God!

By his mighty power at work within us, he is able to accomplish infinitely more than we would ever dare to ask or hope. May he be given glory in the church and in Christ Jesus forever and ever through endless ages. Amen. (Ephesians 3:16–21, NLT)

True Foundations
Living Truth for Lifelong Growth

Begin a "Christianity 101" Process

The three integrated courses described below and on the
following pages will help you reveal the heart of God
and lead your people through a spiritual formation process.

REVEALING THE **GOD OF REDEMPTION**
WHO GAVE HIS LIFE TO REDEEM US

FOR CHILDREN	FOR YOUTH	FOR ADULTS
Is Christ Really God?	**Is Christ Really God?**	**Is Christ Really God?**
The Real Truth about Why Jesus Came	A Personal Encounter with the Transforming Christ	How to Lead your Youth to a Personal Encounter with the Transforming Christ

Uncovering the deep meaning of God's redemptive heart will open our hearts and minds
to who God truly is and prompts us to commit our lives to him.

Receiving the God of Redemption leads us to live a life of:

• Faith in God   • Worship of God   • Prayer to God

REVEALING THE **GOD OF RELATIONSHIPS**
WHO GAVE HIS SPIRIT & THE WORD TO BECOME INTIMATE WITH US

FOR CHILDREN	FOR YOUTH	FOR ADULTS
Is the Bible Personally from God?	**Christ Up Close & Personal**	**Christ Up Close & Personal**
The Real Truth about Living Like Jesus	The Real Truth about God's Spirit and His Word	How to Lead your Youth to Discover the Real Truth about God's Spirit and His Word

God gave us his Spirit and his Word to empower us to become more and more like Christ.

Embracing the God of Relationships leads us to live a life of:

• Loving Others as Christ Loves Us   • Making Godly Choices

REVEALING THE **GOD OF RESTORATION**
WHO CONQUERED DEATH & GAVE US HIS CHURCH TO RECLAIM HIS KINGDOM

FOR CHILDREN	FOR YOUTH	FOR ADULTS
Will There Really Be a Perfect World?	**Christ Will Make All Things Right**	**Christ Will Make All Things Right**
The Real Truth about a Recreated Heaven & Earth	Your Mission and True Sense of Belonging in Life	How to Lead your Youth to Embrace Their Mission & True Sense of Belonging

God is on a mission and has given to us (his church) the same mission of reclaiming lost souls
and bringing them into the family of God. *(This course is in development and will be released in 2008.
Not pictured on the following pages).*

Accepting the Mission of the God of Restoration leads us to live a life of:

• Spiritual Warfare   • Spiritual Reproduction

                 Appendix

True Foundations
Living Truth for Lifelong Growth

Revealing the **God of Redemption**
Who Gave His Life to Redeem Us

13-SESSION *ADULT* GROUP COURSE

Is Christ Really God?

This 5-part DVD series and 8-session Interactive Group Course equips adults with solid answers for who Christ really is and how to lead young people into a transformed relationship with God. The DVD series features Josh McDowell in each session and comes with a comprehensive Leaders Guide. The 8-session Interactive Group Course has a self-contained Leaders Guide with reproducible handouts for group participants. (This is a revised course previously titled *Belief Matters.*)   (Available Aug. 2006)

13-SESSION *YOUTH* GROUP COURSE

Is Christ Really God?

This youth edition 5-part DVD series combines a powerful message, compelling media illustrations, and captivating group activities to convince your students that only Christ as the true Son of God can transform our "dead lives" into a meaningful life in relationship with him. The 8-session Interactive Group Course guides them in how to live out their devotion to God, leading them to a face-to-face encounter with Christ and helping them experience a committed relationship with him. (This is a revised course previously titled *The Revolt.*)   (Available Aug. 2006)

8-SESSION *CHILDREN'S* GROUP COURSE

Is Christ Really God?

These workbooks for children grades 1-3 and 4-6 present foundational truth of Christ's deity and why he came to earth. Written in simple terms, they enable you to lead your children into a transformed relationship with Christ. The comprehensive Leaders Guide is for both the younger and older children's workbooks. Each child is to receive a workbook. (This is a revised course previously titled *True or False.*)   (Available Aug. 2006)

Living a life of faith, worship and prayer to God.
Start today at www.truefoundations.com

Appendix   188

True Foundations
Living Truth for Lifelong Growth

Revealing the **God of Relationships**
Who Gave His Spirit and the Word
to Become Intimate with Us

13-SESSION *ADULT* GROUP COURSE

Christ Up Close & Personal.

This 5-part DVD series and 8-session Interactive Group Course equips adults with a clear understanding of the purpose of the Holy Spirit and his Word. Sessions featuring Josh McDowell, with accompanying Leaders Guide containing reproducible handouts, leads your group to discover the key to instilling Christlike living in their young people. (Available Aug. 2006)

13-SESSION *YOUTH* GROUP COURSE

Christ Up Close & Personal.

With dynamic media illustrations and group activities, this youth edition 5-part DVD series drives home a compelling message: it is impossible to live the Christian life without the presence of the Holy Spirit and knowledge of God's Word. The 8-session Interactive Group Course leads students to love others and make right choices in the power of God's Spirit.

(Available Aug. 2006)

8-SESSION *CHILDREN'S* GROUP COURSE

Is the Bible Personally from God?

These workbooks for children grades 1-3 and 4-6 deliver a powerful message on how God's Spirit enables them to live by his Word in relationship with others. Children will learn how to yield to the Holy Spirit and how that makes both God and them very happy.

(Available Aug. 2006)

Living a life of making godly choices and loving others in Christlikeness.
Start today at www.truefoundations.com.

Helping You to Lead This Generation
through a Biblically-Based Spiritual Formation Process

ADDITIONAL RESOURCES FOR *ADULTS*

- ***The Last Christian Generation*** – In this book, the defining message of Josh's ministry, he offers a fresh revelation of the heart of God and 7 lifelong responses of a true follower of Christ.

- ***The Relational Word*** – This book reveals relationship as the true purpose of God's Word and shows how to make Christ come alive in the lives of the next generation. (Available Aug. 2006)

- ***Beyond Belief to Convictions*** – In this book Josh goes beyond just giving us reasons to believe; he shows how our beliefs are to be lived out in relationship with others.

- ***In Search of Certainty*** – We discover in this book evidence that not only is God real and truth absolute, but that trusting in him provides certainty that life has true meaning and fulfillment.

ADDITIONAL RESOURCES FOR *YOUTH*

- ***The Truth Twisters*** – A Novel-Plus that will captivate students with the compelling story of an entire youth group that comes face-to-face with the life changing power of the Holy Spirit and his Word. (Available Aug. 2006)

- ***The Deceivers*** – This Novel-Plus reveals in dramatic fashion that unless Christ is who he claimed to be–the true Son of God–then his offer to redeem us and provide meaning to life can't be real.

- ***Youth Devotions 2*** – This 365-daily devotional arms young people with a spiritual defense that will help them combat today's godless culture.

ADDITIONAL RESOURCES FOR *CHILDREN*

- ***The Great Treasure Quest*** – What is the real purpose of the Bible and who reveals its hidden secrets to us? In this easy-to-read book to children ages 7-11, unlocking the treasure of God's Word becomes an adventurous quest. They will discover how to yield to God's Spirit and obey his words. (Available Aug. 2006)

- ***Children Demand a Verdict*** – Children need clear and direct answers to their questions about God, the Bible, sin, death, etc. Designed for children ages 7-11, this question-and-answer book tackles 77 tough issues with clarity and relevance.

- ***Family Devotions 2*** – This 365-day family devotional provides younger and older children the opportunity to gather around God's Word and learn that serving him is about loving one another and allowing others to see God's love through us.

Contact your Christian supplier to obtain these resources
or **visit www.truefoundations.com.**

True Foundations
Living Truth for Lifelong Growth

Other Ministries that Can Help You

INTIMATE LIFE MINISTRIES

David Ferguson and the Intimate Life Ministries (ILM) team of Austin, Texas can serve you through training and resources. They are primarily focused on providing a support network for ministers (pastors and youth workers), ministries, and Christian leaders.

ILM has developed very effective intergenerational resources, training, and seminar/training events for ministers, such as the "Galatians 6:6" and "Servant Church" retreats. To learn more visit **www.GreatCommandment.net**. For ILM's Center for Relational Care go to **www.relationalcare.org** or call 1-800-881-1808.

SONLIFE MINISTRIES

A youth worker training and church growth service focusing on fulfilling the Great Commission. Visit **www.sonlife.com**.

NATIONAL NETWORK OF YOUTH MINISTRIES

An excellent ministry to get you connected with other youth ministers in your area and gain from their experience. Visit **www.youthworkers.net**.

JESUS FOCUSED YOUTH MINISTRY

A training and resource ministry to youth workers. Visit **www.reach-out.org**.

DARE 2 SHARE MINISTRIES

A training ministry to equip Christian teens to share their faith with courage, clarity and compassion. Visit **www.dare2share.org**.

Our goal is to help you reach yours.
Visit www.truefoundations.com.

Appendix

Notes

Chapter One

1. George Barna, *Real Teens* (Ventura, CA: Regal Books, 2001), 136.
2. Nehemiah Institute, Inc. *PEERS Trend Chart and Explanation*, (Lexington, KY: www.nehemiahinstitute.com, 2004).
3. Barna Research Group, "Life Goals of American Teens," study commissioned by Josh McDowell Ministry (Ventura, CA: The Barna Research Group, Ltd., 2001), 6.
4. Ibid, 8.
5. Ibid, 4.
6. Barna Research Group, "Third Millennium Teens" (Ventura, CA: The Barna Research Group, Ltd., 1999), 51.
7. Ibid, 65.
8. Ibid, 43.
9. Josephson Institute of Ethics: "The Ethics of American Youth," (2002ReportCard@www.josephsoninstitue.org).
10. George Barna, *Think Like Jesus* (Minneapolis: Baker Books, 2003), 26.

11. George Barna, *The State of the Church: 2005* (Ventura, CA: The Barna Research Group, Ltd., 2005), 51.

Chapter Two

1. Josh D. McDowell and Bob Hostetler, *Right From Wrong* (Nashville: Word, 1994), 263.
2. Jerry Adler, "In Search of the Spiritual," *Newsweek*, September 5, 2005, 48-49.
3. Barna Research Group, "Third Millennium Teens" (Ventura, CA: The Barna Research Group, Ltd., 1999), 49.
4. Ibid, 49.

Chapter Three

1. Jim Leffel, "Our New Challenge: Postmodernism," *The Death of Truth*, ed. Dennis McCallum (Minneapolis: Bethany House, 1996), 35.
2. Barna Research Group, "Third Millennium Teens" (Ventura, CA: The Barna Research Group, Ltd., 1999), 47.
3. Ibid, 44.

Chapter Four

1. "Top 100 Books Listed in OCLC Database," in *University of North Dakota Chester Fritz Library News*, Fall 1999, Vol. 9, Issue 2, 2 (http://www.und.edu/dept/library/Libpub/Libnews/fall299.pdf).
2. Rick Richardson, "Eight Urgent Questions by Today's Generation," (http://www.getchurch.org/inside/01-04.)

3. Barna Research Group, "Third Millennium Teens" (Ventura, CA: The Barna Research Group, Ltd., 1999), 44.
4. Millard J.Erickson, *Christian Theology*, 2nd. ed. (Grand Rapids: Baker, 1998), 45.
5. Notebook, "Verbatim," *Time*, July 18, 2005, 13.

Chapter Five

1. Barna Research Group, "Third Millennium Teens" (Ventura, CA: The Barna Research Group, Ltd., 1999), 63.
2. Ibid, 18.
3. Ibid, 18.
4. Ibid, 39.
5. Ibid, 16.
6. Rick Warren, *The Purpose Driven Church* (Grand Rapids: Zondervan, 1996), 191.
7. Barna Research Group, "Third Millennium Teens," 66.
8. Ibid, 37.
9. Ibid, 37.
10. Ibid, 68.
11. BeyondBelief.com, March 2003 Newsletter Survey (Dallas: Josh McDowell Ministry, 2003).
12. BeyondBelief.com, March 2003 Newsletter Survey (Dallas: Josh McDowell Ministry, 2003).

Chapter Six

1. Barna Research Group, "Third Millennium Teens" (Ventura, CA: The Barna Research Group, Ltd., 1999), 39.

2. Christian Smith, *Soul Searching: The Religious and Spiritual Lives of American Teenagers* (New York: Oxford University Press, 2005), 89.

Chapter Seven

1. Adapted from Michael Strassfeld's *The Jewish Holidays* (New York: Harper Collins Publishers, 1985), 6, 23, 25.

Chapter Eight

1. Adapted from Josh D. McDowell, Bob Hostetler, and David H. Bellis, *Beyond Belief to Convictions* (Wheaton, IL: Tyndale House Publishers, 2002), 83-85.
2. Adapted from Josh McDowell and Bob Hostetler, *Right From Wrong* (Nashville: Word, 1994), 87-89.
3. Adapted from "To My Dear Husband," (Cleveland: American Greetings, 2005).
4. Isaac Watts, "When I Survey the Wondrous Cross," (Newbury Park, CA: Lexicon Music Inc., 1976), 156.

Chapter Nine

1. Adapted from Josh McDowell, Bob Hostetler, and David H. Bellis, *Beyond Belief to Convictions* (Wheaton, IL: Tyndale House Publishers, 2002), 189-191.
2. Rick Warren, *The Purpose Driven Life* (Grand Rapids: Zondervan, 2002), 17.
3. Barna Research Group, "Third Millennium Teens" (Ventura, CA: The Barna Research Group, Ltd., 1999), 44.
4. Ibid., 43.

5. Josh McDowell and Bob Hostetler, *The Truth Slayers* (Nashville: Word Publishing, 1995), 129-132.

Chapter Ten

1. "The Churched Youth Study" (Dallas: Josh McDowell Ministry, 1994), 69.
2. Cecilia Goodnow, "Is It Teen Angst or Depression," *Seattle Post-Intelligencer*, October 28, 2002.
3. Ibid.
4. David Ferguson, *The Never Alone Church* (Wheaton, IL: Tyndale House Publishers, 1998), 13.
5. C. S. Lewis, *Mere Christianity* (New York: Macmillan, 1943), 36.
6. Rick Warren, *The Purpose Driven Life* (Grand Rapids: Zondervan, 2002), 285.

Chapter Eleven

1. George Barna, *The State of the Church: 2005* (Ventura, CA: The Barna Group, 2005), 25.
2. Ibid., 21.
3. George Barna, *Think Like Jesus* (Minneapolis: Baker Books, 2003), 26.

Chapter Twelve

1. George Barna, *The State of the Church: 2005* (Ventura, CA: The Barna Group, 2005), 12 and 14.
2. Os Guiness, *The American Hour* (New York: The Free Press, 1993), 84.

About the Authors

JOSH MCDOWELL never intended to be a defender of the Christian faith. In fact, his goal was just the opposite. As a skeptic at Kellogg College in Michigan, he was challenged by a group of Christian students to examine intellectually the claims of Christianity. He accepted the challenge and set out to prove that Christ's claims to be God and the historical reliability of Scripture could be neither trusted nor accurately verified. The evidence he discovered changed the course of his life. He discovered that the Bible was the most historically reliable document of all antiquity and that Christ's claim that he was God was true. That brought him to the inescapable conclusion that Christ loved him and died to redeem him. Josh then trusted in Christ as the Son of God and his personal Savior.

Josh transferred to Wheaton College and completed a bachelor's degree in language. He went on to receive a master's degree in theology from Talbot Theological Seminary in California. In 1964, he joined the staff of Campus Crusade for Christ (CCC) and eventually became an international traveling representative for the ministry, focusing primarily on issues facing young people.

Josh has spoken to more than ten million young people in eighty-four countries, including more than 700 university and college campuses. He has authored or co-authored more than one hundred books and workbooks with more than forty-two million in print worldwide. Josh's most popular works are *The New Evidence That Demands a Verdict, More Than a Carpenter,* the *Right from Wrong* book, and *Beyond Belief to Convictions.*

Josh has been married to Dottie for more than thirty-four years and has four children. Josh and Dottie live in Dana Point, California.

DAVE BELLIS is a writer, producer, and ministry consultant focusing on ministry planning and product development. He has pioneered an interactive video and workbook educational design used by more than 100,000 churches and small groups worldwide. For over twenty-nine years, Dave has directed Josh McDowell's many campaigns, developing more than 100 products. He and his wife, Becky, live in Copley, Ohio and have two grown children and six grandchildren.